Additional Praise for
The Respectful Leader. . .

"*The Respectful Leader* teaches you more, in 90 minutes, about respectful, conscious leadership and its powerful impact on business success than you might ever learn in a lifetime."

Kevin Rafferty,
The Conscious Leaders Coach, author, *Wake Up,*
Get Real, Be Happy—Becoming Your Authentic Self

"Few business leaders appreciate that respect is the foundation of any high-performing organization. With respectful leadership, all of the other leadership tools and techniques are effective; without it, they all break down. Gregg Ward is the guru of respect and he nails it in this powerful, engaging, and useful fable."

John N. Kohut,
Chief Operating Officer, Orison

"Ward skillfully summarizes the importance of strong interpersonal relations—so often underappreciated—in the workplace. His story makes it crystal clear how taking the time to improve your skills at respect affects not only the bottom line, but also your staff's loyalty, commitment, and enthusiasm."

Eric Cornwell, M.D.,
Physician, HR, Satisfaction and Diversity,
The Kaiser Permanente Medical Group

"A powerful and impactful read! Best business fable I've read since *Death by Meeting*. With practical and easily remembered rules of the respectful road, Gregg Ward provides all the information you need to create an environment of respect, trust, teamwork, and high performance, both in your business and for your family."

Joseph C. Adan,
Public Sector Department Head,
Captain, U.S. Navy (Ret.)

"*The Respectful Leader* is a refreshing antidote to what's wrong in today's rude, rushed, and me-first workplace, and a practical guide for those who want to create a civil and courteous culture."

Christopher Witt,
author, *Real Leaders Don't Do PowerPoint*

"This intriguing story clearly illuminates one of the biggest challenges in today's workplace—the overwhelming lack of respect by people at all levels, and particularly by leaders. But it doesn't have to be this way! Being respectful is simple—if you reach back and remember the lessons your parents taught you about how to treat other people, then you're halfway there. Ward's book provides a useful framework and easy-to-follow guidelines that will take you the rest of the way. *The Respectful Leader* will allow you to change your culture, change your company, and even change yourself."

Milton N. Green, Jr.,
Director of People & Culture, Renovate America

"*The Respectful Leader* offers great, practical insights and techniques on how to build a respectful—and successful—organization."

Christopher Aaron,
Director, Comcast Corporation

"Ward is right on target with *The Respectful Leader*. Finally, an easy-to-read and incredibly useful book on the real power of respect and respectful leadership."

Phil Dixon,
Founder and CEO, Academy of
Brain-Based Leadership

"*The Respectful Leader* is a clever and practical book; a must-read for anyone who is a leader as well as anyone who trains or coaches leaders. The examples that Ward uses for building respect within your company will hit home for anyone who reads this compelling book."

Sally Daniel,
President and CEO, The Sally Daniel
Training Group, Inc.

"Respectful leadership is a business imperative for building a trust-based, collaborative, and effective organization. This book is extremely useful for leaders who want to set an overall tone of respect, as well as to mentor and coach their staff. A great read."

**Robert J. Makar,
Partner (ret.), Booz Allen Hamilton**

"Extraordinarily valuable lessons in this book! They sure don't teach you this stuff in business school. *The Respectful Leader* is compelling and practical, while also being a quick, engaging, and easy read."

**Mark Schall,
Business and Executive Coach**

"This story provides a compelling, 'real-world' example of the business challenges that can result from having little or no respect in your workplace. Fortunately, Ward provides practical, easy-to-follow advice on how to turn things around. A must-read for every leader!

**Catherine Mattice,
author, *BACK OFF! Your Kick-Ass Guide
to Ending Bullying at Work***

"The greatest leaders make respectful leadership look easy—a skill often mastered through experience. This book offers valuable leadership lessons in an easy-to-read parable and provides simple methods for influencing others without intimidation. Grimace as the new CEO makes all of the classic leadership mistakes you'll never want to go through and cheer when he transforms into the respectful leader."

**Matthew Rivaldi,
Business Faculty, San Diego State University**

The

RESPECTFUL LEADER

Seven Ways to Influence Without Intimidation

A Business Fable

GREGG WARD

With WALTER G. MEYER

Cover Design: Wiley
Cover Image: © Marc Dufresne/iStockphoto

For general information on our other products and services or for technical support, please contact our Customer Care Department within the United States at (800) 762-2974, outside the United States at (317) 572-3993 or fax (317) 572-4002.

Wiley also publishes its books in a variety of electronic formats. Some content that appears in print may not be available in electronic books. For more information about Wiley products, visit our website at www.wiley.com.

Library of Congress Cataloging-in-Publication Data:

Library of Congress Cataloging-in-Publication Data has been applied for and is on file with the Library of Congress.
ISBN 978-1-119-28156-6 (hardback); ISBN 978-1-119-28157-3 (epdf);
ISBN 978-1-119-28158-0 (epub)

Printed in the United States of America

10 9 8 7 6 5 4 3 2 1

Dedicated to my father, Gene Ward—sportswriter, outdoorsman, poet—who treated everyone with respect.

Contents

x   Contents

Introduction

As my colleagues and I travel around the world giving speeches and leading seminars, we keep hearing the same lament from employees, managers, even leadership. Just about everyone feels that there's more and more disrespect going on in our workplaces than ever before. We're hearing that common courtesy isn't common practice; that employees feel bullied, ignored, and undervalued; and that senior management considers them disposable when times get tough or priorities change. Numerous employee surveys and organizational culture studies support these perceptions. Maybe you're experiencing this, too?

So why is this? Why are people feeling so disrespected?

Well, it could be that rapid globalization is mushing together diverse groups of people faster and more intensely, and that what is considered acceptable and tolerable behavior in one culture may be considered disrespectful and intolerable in another.

It could also be that the ever-increasing frenzy and complexity of business, the shift to the freelance and "gig" economy, and continuous economic uncertainty cause people to shove courtesy aside because they're afraid of losing time, opportunities, and resources. There's no question that operating from a mindset of scarcity can quickly drive a normally respectful person to be extraordinarily rude.

Ambition, competitiveness, and managers with so-called "Type A" personalities—who are determined to win at any cost—can also contribute to sustaining disrespectful work cultures where decency and caring are considered synonymous with weakness and ineffectuality. Additionally, "competitive busy-ness," the tendency to take on overwhelming amounts of work in order to increase a sense of self-importance and the boss's perception of one's value, can also be a handy excuse for rudeness.

Still another factor contributing to all of this disrespect may be our ever-expanding love affair with technology—smart phones, tablets, laptops, and apps for every possible need or want—leading us to skip traditional human interaction in favor of a text, chat, or email. How many times have we received emotionally loaded emails from someone down the hall, or on another floor, about an issue that could easily have been resolved with a quick phone call or face-to-face? How many meetings have we been in with people who are supposed to be paying attention and contributing, but they're constantly being distracted by their smart phones? Everyone agrees that these are disrespectful behaviors, and yet most of us say nothing, especially if our bosses are the culprits.

That brings us to this book. After more than two decades of studying and learning about respect and disrespect while consulting and leading training programs for some of the world's most prestigious companies, non-profits, and government agencies, my colleagues and I—not to mention many top consultants and organization development experts—have become convinced that creating and maintaining a work culture of respect and Respectful Leadership are absolute business imperatives.

Respectful Leadership means treating everyone—regardless of rank, status, or position—with the same genuine regard and consideration that you would like them to give you. It means being the first to offer respect to others, even strangers, and behaving in a respect-worthy way. It means getting your "emotional shift" (more on this later) together when things go wrong. It means acknowledging and honoring others; consistently looking for qualities in others to respect; nipping disrespect in the bud, respectfully; and fully apologizing for disrespectful behavior.

Although Respectful Leadership as an idea may seem like a warm and fuzzy, the measureable results are hard to dismiss: they include increased loyalty, respect, trust, collaboration, and productivity; fewer complaints, conflicts, and lawsuits; and an energizing sense throughout the entire organization that each one of us can be wholly successful in whatever we're doing while still behaving, and being treated, like decent human beings. Bottom line: the human and business case for Respectful Leadership is undeniable and irrefutable.

But for many years we struggled with a basic question: How do we make that business case for Respectful Leadership in a way that everyone can understand and want to buy into?

The answer is to tell a short, easy-to-read story about people and situations that are familiar to most, if not all of us. It's very likely you'll know and work with people who are similar to the people in our fable. And it's likely that their behaviors, and the challenges they're facing, are also very familiar to you. It's that familiarity—that sense of "Yup, that's kind of how we are" feeling—that will allow you to make the human and business case for Respectful Leadership for yourself.

It's our sincere hope that you will find this story, and the concepts, tools, and techniques we outline within it, to be truly useful in helping you and your organization understand how powerful, effective, and rewarding Respectful Leadership can be.

PART

I

The Fable

1

Settling In

It was 7:55 a.m. on a beautiful Southern California Monday, and Des Hogan, the brand-new chief executive officer of COR-Med Corporation, leaned back in his new executive chair, put his hands behind his head, his feet up on his desk, and mentally patted himself on the back.

Well, buddy, he thought, you've really made it: CEO of a $35M company before you turn 40; a fabulous, loving wife; two wonderful kids—well, one, anyway—a son, and also one moody teenage daughter; a new company-leased "Beemer" parked just outside; a washboard stomach; and a small, but growing slice of the medical device market in the United States and overseas. Life couldn't be much sweeter.

A text from his wife Laura came in: "Good luck! So proud of you! Love, ME." After texting "Thank You!!" he made a mental note: *give wonderful gift to wonderful wife because she's always encouraging me to "go for it."* You wouldn't be here, he reminded himself, without her.

And "luck"? Yeah, Des thought, luck may have played a part in landing this gig. But mostly, he felt that he'd been put in this position on his merits, because of who he was and what he'd done. He didn't necessarily think he needed a lot of luck to be successful from here on; he just needed determination.

Sure, he'd only been tapped for this job ten days ago. And yes, the previous CEO and CFO had been terminated under mysterious circumstances, leaving the company in much worse shape than they'd found it in. In fact, he really didn't know much at all about the inner workings of the place other than the financials were out of whack, and he wasn't sure why.

But those were details, he thought, nothing he couldn't handle. Besides, he was about to have his first meeting with his leadership team to start going full speed on the turnaround. I'll figure this thing out, he assured himself, I can do this!

Then his desk phone rang. Des deliberately didn't answer it, assuming his assistant Rita would pick up. But it kept on ringing. Perplexed, he called out of his office door into the reception area: "Rita, can you pick up? Rita?" No answer. After a moment of wondering whether he was going to have issues with his executive assistant, he shrugged his shoulders and picked up the handset: "Des Hogan here."

"Des? What the hell are you doing answering your own phone?" It was Des's boss, Chuck Morton, the president and CEO of Arellus International, COR-Med's parent company. Arellus was a massive global operation valued at $3.5 billion, with over 40,000 employees worldwide. Chuck had picked Des for this job, taking a big risk by pulling him out of a COO slot at another Arellus subsidiary. He'd specifically warned Des that he would keep a close eye on him.

"Oh, hey, Chuck. I was just wondering that myself." Des tried to sound unconcerned: "Looks like my assistant's gone missing for a moment. No problem."

"Well, don't go letting your staff take advantage of you, got it? Anyway, I wanted to be the very first person to call you on your very first day in the CEO's chair. How's it going so far?"

Des thought for a second, wondering what Chuck would want to hear. Realizing that he needed to impress his boss, even though he hadn't even touched his feet to the ground, he lied: "Great! I'm already kicking ass and taking names."

"Outstanding," replied Chuck, expansively. "That's the ticket."

Des inwardly sighed with relief. Chuck had made it crystal clear that COR-Med was in trouble, in need of a serious intervention. This was partly the result of the incompetence of the previous CEO Chuck had installed right after Arellus bought out COR-Med's founders two years ago. According to Chuck, Des's predecessor wasn't tough enough on the employees, didn't cut expenses deeply enough, or ramp up development or production fast enough and, in general, was missing a spine.

Chuck continued without pausing for breath: "I don't think I need to tell you again how important it is that you turn that place around as fast as you can."

"No, sir, you don't. I'm on it." Des suddenly noticed that his office seemed very warm and that he'd starting sweating.

"Good to hear. Not to put too fine a point on it, but I will anyway. I'm giving you six months, maybe eight, to show real progress, especially on raising revenues and cutting costs, understood?"

Des swallowed silently but hard, and his upbeat mood burst like a soap bubble. That's not a lot of time, he thought. Still, he was pretty confident in himself: "I can do it, boss."

"OK, good, because if you don't, you'll be gone as fast as the guy you just replaced, got it? Sorry to be so blunt, but this is business."

Des took a deep breath and replied in his most serious, mature, and deepest CEO voice: "Absolutely. I understand."

"Good! Well then, have fun!" Chuck hung up without saying goodbye. Des exhaled very slowly through his lips, like a horse, greatly relieved to be done with that particular call.

Rita popped her head in the door. "I'm sorry to interrupt, Mr. Hogan. . . ."

"Rita, where've you been?" he snapped a bit too harshly, venting his frustration with Chuck on her. "I had to answer my own frickin' phone."

"I'm really sorry, Mr. Hogan," she said, looking genuinely crestfallen, "I was in the restroom and when I came back you were on the phone with Mr. Morton. So I went to tell everyone in the conference room that you'd be there as soon as you were done."

"Right!" Des said, jumping up and acting as if he hadn't been completely distracted by Chuck's call. "OK, good."

"My pleasure, Mr. Hogan," she said, her mood brightening.

Des grabbed his cell phone and notes for his meeting with his leadership team and headed out of his office. On his way into the hall, he stopped. "Um, Rita, why do you keep calling me Mr. Hogan?"

"Well," she stammered, "I just thought, out of respect, that I should."

"OK, that's great. But from now on, just call me Des. OK?"

"Yes, Mr. . . . um . . . Des."

"Great." Des charged energetically out of the reception area and turned left in the hallway heading away from the lobby. Glancing at the walls and ceiling as he walked, he flashed back to his first impressions of the building when he visited a few weeks before. It was old and tired, with furnishings that looked like they were bought during the Reagan Administration. Disappointed, he'd immediately asked Rita to order a new executive chair and made a mental note to consider selling the place and relocating down to where the real action was, near the University of California at San Diego, surrounded by a rash of biotech and medical device companies.

Then he heard Rita's voice calling down the hallway, "Excuse me, um . . . Des?"

"What's up?" he called back over his shoulder without stopping.

"Actually, the main conference room is back this way, to the right and toward the front entrance."

"Oops!" Des did a quick 180 and headed back the other way. But he hadn't even gone five steps when he heard loud, angry shouting coming from the conference room.

What the heck?

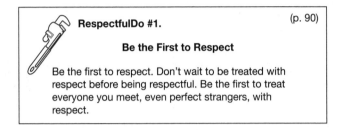

RespectfulDo #1.

(p. 90)

Be the First to Respect

Be the first to respect. Don't wait to be treated with respect before being respectful. Be the first to treat everyone you meet, even perfect strangers, with respect.

2

Meeting the Team

Des stopped just outside the conference room door and peered in, hoping to get a sense of what all the yelling was about before he made his entrance. He was completely startled by the amount of anger he felt radiating from the people in the room.

A Filipino-American woman with short, straight, brown hair—Janet Bantay, COR-Med's chief talent officer—was standing with both hands flat on the table in front of her, her head jutting up and directly toward a tall, balding, thin man in his mid-40s, wearing rimless, round glasses over a long, sharp nose. This was Peter Durso, the head of R&D, known to everyone as "Spec," which was short for "specifications." Spec was mirroring Janet's posture right back at her, even down to the jutting head, like bulls staring each other down. It was obvious that each was furious with the other.

Behind them at the table sat Mateo Torres, COR-Med's executive vice president of sales, with his head down, staring at a smart phone in his lap. He was the youngest of the group—perhaps in his late 20s or early 30s. He had meticulously coifed brown hair, a chiseled jaw covered in trendy stubble, and was dressed snappily in a herringbone sports jacket, crisp black slacks, and a light blue dress shirt with French cuffs and silver cufflinks. Mateo, whom everyone called "Matt," seemed surprisingly untroubled by the tension in the room.

At the back, behind the others and next to the picture window, Des spotted Karl Schneider, head of IT, whose expanding middle and completely grey hair marked him as the oldest member of the leadership team. He was standing, hunched over, with his hands deep in the pockets of his khakis, staring out at the mountains off to the east. Des got the sense from his body language that if the window had been the kind that opened, Karl would have leapt out of it at that very moment.

Des was well aware that this was in no way a "complete" leadership team. In fact, it was barely a skeleton crew, missing at least three key players, like a COO, a CFO, and a head of marketing. But, like Des's predecessor, those folks had either been summarily dispatched by Chuck, had their roles folded into someone else's, or had left of their own volition. When he'd told Des he was naming him CEO, Chuck made it clear that tight finances dictated that that was the way the C-Suite had to be configured until COR-Med made real, measureable progress.

To make his first morning even more challenging, Des had met the remaining players only once, during his all-too-brief walkthrough with Chuck ten days before. He'd been more than a little nervous, and Chuck's outsized personality was so overbearing, that the tour was nothing but a blur of Des following his boss around like an anxious puppy. As a result, Des had no sense of any of the individual personalities of his leadership team.

He also noticed that the conference room—which was very large with high ceilings and exposed brickwork—was even hotter than his office. Didn't the air conditioning work anywhere in this place? And when was the last time they changed the carpet? It looked as bad as it smelled.

"You just refuse to get it, and that's all there is to it!" snarled Janet, snapping Des back into the present.

"I get it just fine!" Spec replied, snarling right back at her. "You're the one who's clueless here!"

Des decided it was time to make his entrance and take control of the situation. So he inhaled deeply, puffed out his chest like a rooster, and strode into the room declaiming: "Hello, everyone. What the heck is going on here?"

Janet and Spec immediately clammed up, pulled back from their fighting stance, and sat down, still staring daggers at each other. Matt looked up from his phone and offered Des an unctuous smile, while Karl just turned around slowly, his hands still stuffed in his pockets, and looked at him with a tired face.

Now, as the new CEO, Des had expected to be respected enough that someone would respond with an actual answer to his question, not just silence. So he asked again, this time in a much more annoyed tone: "I asked what is going on here?!"

Janet and Spec continued to stare angrily at each other, and the stony looks Matt and Karl gave him made it clear that they weren't going to be the first to speak.

Finally, Spec broke the silence. "Our 'chief talent officer' here," he said derisively, indicating Janet with a nod of his head, "keeps tells me that I have to make do with the engineers I've got, which isn't enough by half."

Janet immediately jumped to her own defense: "And the head of R&D doesn't seem to understand the meaning of the term 'hiring freeze.'"

"Oh, I understand it fine," Spec snapped back viciously. "But what you don't get is that without those engineers, we're gonna lose our biggest client and," Spec continued, pausing after each word and air-stabbing his finger at her for emphasis, "We . . . Are . . . Out . . . Of . . . Business."

Whoa!, thought Des, yes Chuck had made it clear that COR-Med was in a tough financial position, but he didn't say that it was on the brink of collapse.

Then Matt piped up: "Stop blowing things out of proportion, will you, Spec? Look, under the circumstances, given our financial situation, we're just going to have to make do with what we've got until Des gets us sorted out."

"Don't give us that shit, Matt. I'm not blowing anything out of proportion. We are in serious trouble, and we all know it," Spec said dismissively, still staring at Janet, who stared right back.

Wow! Des wasn't shy about cursing; he'd done his share over the years. But he was a little surprised that a subordinate would curse in a very first meeting with the new CEO. Also, given the tension in the room and not knowing Matt at all, Des couldn't figure out whether his remark about "making do" was sarcasm or just an attempt to curry favor with the new boss.

It was time to take charge, he thought. "OK, everyone just calm down," Des commanded.

"How exactly can I be calm," Janet retorted, "when I'm constantly being accused of not doing my job?!"

"You're not doing your job, dammit!" Spec shouted.

"And you are? Seriously?!" Janet shot back.

"Guys, guys, guys!" Matt interjected, throwing his hands out and patting the air. "Des just got here."

Spec turned to Des icily: "Well, welcome to COR-Med." Then he snapped back to Janet: "OK, forget about who's doing what or not. Just what the hell are we supposed to say on tomorrow's call with Avi Kumar about why we're so far behind?"

"We?" Janet demanded of him incredulously. "Who's we?"

"You know damn well that 'we' means 'me.' Avi's going to want to know our status on his prototype. And I'm just sick and tired of having to take the blame for everything that's going wrong around here!"

Des looked questioningly at Matt, asking, "Remind me, Avi Kumar?"

"CEO of Emperor Health in Oakland," Matt said flatly, leaning in his chair toward Des. "Basically," he continued with a resigned sigh and shake of his head, "R&D is way behind on their latest job, and Avi's not going to be a happy camper when he hears about it."

"Got it," said Des, remembering that Emperor was one of COR-Med's biggest customers. Uh-oh.

Spec clarified: "We're late on Avi's prototype because Janet isn't bringing in enough engineers fast enough to get it done anywhere near on time."

"That's bull, Spec, and you know it!" Janet countered fiercely. "There's no budget! You can't expect people to volunteer to work for free! This isn't a freakin' startup."

Spec turned to Des. "The only thing I know is we're about to seriously piss off and maybe even lose one of our biggest customers. If that happens, we are in big trouble, and I sure as hell am not going to take the blame for it."

Des turned to Janet, trying to sound decisive. "Janet, what do *you* think we should tell them?"

She shook her head in disbelief. "There's that 'we' again. I'm sorry Des, but it's not my responsibility to come up with what R&D should say to Avi Kumar." Then she turned to Matt: "But if Spec's too chicken, maybe it should come from Sales."

Everyone looked at Matt, who reacted as if he'd pre-planned his next remark. "Normally, I would agree," he said, putting his hands up as if to push the idea away.

"Yeah, right," Spec hissed sarcastically under his breath. He shot a look at Janet: "And I'm not scared of Avi or anyone else."

"Whatever," Janet murmured dismissively, leaning back in her chair.

"But," Matt countered, ignoring them both, "considering how far behind we are, whatever gets said to Avi should probably come directly from the CEO."

"Now hold on a second," Des blurted out, feeling ambushed. "I'm not exactly up to speed on this."

Spec turned quickly to Des. "Well, that's understandable. I'll fill you in about it later today, alone. There's no point in doing that now since I can't say anything without these people blaming me for everything. So, excuse me, I just need to go." Without waiting for permission, Spec quickly stood up and strode from the room. Des was dumbfounded. He just walked out of my meeting!

Janet shook her head again and sighed, as if to say "typical." She pointed at the door and loudly whispered to Des, "Incredibly . . . disrespectful . . . pain . . . in . . . the . . . butt."

Apparently Spec hadn't gone very far because they all heard him yell from the hall, "I heard that!"

"Ooops!" Janet said insincerely, and loudly enough to make sure he'd heard. She took a breath, turned to Des, and extended her hand. "Anyway, welcome aboard, Des. I sure hope you can hang in there longer than the last guy."

"Thanks, I guess." Des shook her hand.

"Would you mind if I take a quick walk for a moment before we go on with the meeting," Janet asked, "just to clear my head?"

Des thought about saying yes, but he didn't have the stomach for more group drama. "That's OK, just come to my office at one o'clock."

Surprised, she backed off, "Oh, well . . . I don't have to take a walk. I can stay."

"No," Des insisted. "Just come to my office at one."

Janet's face sank. She sighed "OK," picked up a binder from the table, and headed for the door. Once there, she glanced back at Des with a confused look and then left slowly, shaking her head as she walked away.

Des, annoyed but focused, turned his attention to Matt, who had his head back down, checking messages on his phone.

"Don't mind them," Matt chirped with a flippancy that didn't seem to fit the seriousness of the moment. "They're always going at it." He looked up from his phone. "Why don't I fill you in, give you a status report?"

"No," replied Des. "I'm postponing this meeting to tomorrow morning at 8 a.m."

"Got it," Matt said with a resigned sigh. "It'll probably be more of the same. But don't worry, dude; I'll have your back."

Arrogant bastard, thought Des. "I can take care of myself," he snapped, not sure which was more annoying, Spec's open disrespect or Matt's fake helpfulness.

Matt dropped the wingman act and snorted, "Sure, OK, of course."

"Come to my office at three today and give me your report then," Des said bluntly.

"Right, will do. See ya." Matt exited quickly, without even acknowledging Karl, still standing alone at the window.

Des turned to look at Karl. "We only met for a second when you were here with Chuck," Karl said, speaking for the first time, "so you probably don't remember me; which isn't all that surprising." He took his hands out of his pockets and came forward. "I'm Karl Schneider, head of IT."

"Of course I remember you," Des lied, shaking Karl's now outstretched hand.

"Well, *that* sure was fun."

Des was in no mood for sarcasm. "Yeah, I guess. Let me ask you a question: Is it always like this?"

"Pretty much," said Karl, resignedly. "Spec and Janet have never been very fond of each other."

"I get that," said Des. "And Matt?" indicating the now empty chair.

"Oh, he doesn't do open combat. He's what my ex-wife calls the 'passive-aggressive type.' Different generation. He kinda makes you feel like you need to take a shower after he's done with you."

"Actually, I could use a shower," Des replied, not quite knowing how to respond to the cutting remark about Matt. "It's hot as hell in here."

"Yeah, it is. The AC's out again. But Grace will fix it soon enough."

For a moment, Des wondered if Karl was making some kind of religious statement, and there was an uncomfortable pause. Then Karl filled the silence. "Look, I'm sorry you had to see this on your first day. Everyone is under a lot of stress. You know, revolving-door CEOs; the cutbacks and layoffs; the delays on the Emperor project, not to mention the other customers' work. Everyone is just really stressed out."

Des wasn't sure how to reply. "Yup, I get it," was all he could say.

"I prepared a short report for you on my group, what's left of it anyway," added Karl. "I can present it to you any time today that works for you."

"OK, how about at 11?"

"Right, sounds good. OK then. I'll see you later. Um . . . I guess I should say 'welcome to COR-Med,' but under the circumstances, I think maybe . . . well, anyway, I'll see ya." He walked out slowly, his hands diving back in his pockets, leaving Des alone.

Des took a deep breath, exhaled noisily, and sank down into a chair to ponder what the heck he was going to do. Half the leadership team walks out of my meeting totally upset, he thought. The other half doesn't seem to care about much of anything and are all but checked out.

Well, at least Des had his answer to the question he'd asked when he walked in the door. What was going on here was a steaming mess of chaos, a whole lot of anger, and a surprising whiff of mutiny. Speaking of steaming, he thought, it's freakin' hot in this building.

Suddenly there was a loud clang from somewhere in the room. It was so loud that Des jumped out of his chair.

"What the hell?! Who's that? Hello?" Looking around, he saw nothing that might make such a sound. But then he spotted a utility closet in the far corner of the room that he hadn't noticed before. He went over to it, approaching it carefully. "Hello?"

The closet door swung open to reveal a short, barrel-shaped woman wearing old, faded blue coveralls covered in grease marks, scuffed black work shoes, and a brown-and-yellow vintage San Diego Padres' ball cap turned backwards. She looked to be no more than 5 feet tall—probably a couple of inches less—and judging from the grey hair jutting out from under her hat and the lines around her mouth and eyes, Des guessed she was in her mid-60s. She was holding a huge, red pipe wrench in her hand and smiling.

"Sorry about that." She indicated the wrench. "This sucker is slippery."

"Who are you?" Des demanded while taking an unconscious step backward to avoid getting dirt on his clothes.

"I'm Gracia Peña, from maintenance. Everyone just calls me Grace." She deliberately put her hands and the wrench behind her back. "You don't want to shake my hand; it's got grease all over it."

So this is who Karl meant by Grace, Des thought. "Have you been there the whole time?" he asked.

"If you mean during your . . . um . . . meeting, then yep, the whole time."

Des noticed she had a way of clipping her words as she spoke, sounding very matter-of-fact, to-the-point. "Why didn't you tell us you were in there?"

"Well," she replied, "there was so much yelling going on, I didn't think anyone would hear me. Besides, I'm no one to worry about. It's just that I need to work in here because the HVAC unit's down again."

"Yeah, I noticed," snorted Des. "This whole place is like an oven."

Grace seemed to take personal offense to this. "It's nothing we can't handle. I'll get it fixed."

"Does it happen a lot?" Des demanded.

"Well, it is an old building."

Des felt she was making excuses. "I know. I've seen it. It's falling apart."

"Well, I don't know about 'falling apart,'" Grace replied earnestly. "The ol' girl been a good place for us all these years. She's still pretty solid; just needs a little tender-loving care, and for people to treat her with respect."

Des made a dubious grunt. Calling a building "ol' girl," he thought. Seriously? He turned to leave.

Grace called after him. "So you're the new CEO?"

"Yup. That's me," he replied over his shoulder, pulling out his cell phone and heading for the door.

"Well," Grace said, "nice to meet you. . . ."

But it was too late; he was gone.

"Ay, Dios mío," Grace said to herself, "Another one," and went back to work.

RespectfulDo #2.   (p. 92)

Practice Regular Respect

Consistently engage in what are universally known as the "common courtesies" such as smiling when you see someone, saying "Good Morning," or "Good Afternoon," "Please," and "Thank You," in a pleasant and genuine manner. Do this with everyone, even strangers you pass in a hallway.

3

Buying Time

"I mean, this is ridiculous!"

It was 9:10 the next morning, and Avi Kumar's voice was booming from the speakerphone on the small, round conference table in Des's office. The leadership team was slumped dejectedly around the table, staring down at the spiderlike device. "You're seriously telling me that you guys have made no progress at all? In three months?! Seriously?!"

"Well, Avi," Des said, trying to sound far more definitive than he felt, "there've been a lot of changes around here, as you know."

"I do know. Chuck Morton called me about it last week," Avi continued. "He promised me that you'd be kicking butt, Des."

"Yes, I am!" Des blurted out, and then realized his team probably wouldn't like hearing this. "I mean I'm doing the best I can. It's just that, well . . . the fact is, I only came on board here in the last few days."

"Well, that shouldn't be my problem," Avi retorted. "COR-Med signed a contract with us over a year ago."

"I understand that, Avi, and we fully intend to honor that contract. It's just that everything changed here very quickly."

"You don't need to say it again," Avi said, clearly annoyed.

"Right, sorry."

Des was more than sorry. He was scared. Yesterday's individual meetings with his leadership team were a tortuous dive into reality: progress on the Emperor prototype was glacial, their other products weren't selling very well, morale was lower than low, and they were hemorrhaging expenses. It had become painfully clear to Des that COR-Med was, as Spec had implied, in deep trouble.

"OK," Avi continued, "so what are you going to do about it?"

Des gulped, took a breath, and said what he'd been dreading saying, "We need to ask you for just a little more time."

"I knew that was coming. How much time?"

"Well, um . . ." stalled Des, looking around the table but deliberately avoiding Spec's warning glare, "five or six weeks, maybe seven."

Spec snapped backwards, threw his hands up in the air, and looked around wildly, his mouth hanging open in shock. He mouthed the words: "That's not what we agreed to say!' But Des stuck his hand up and turned back to the speakerphone. "I'm really sorry to ask this from you, Avi."

There was a moment of silence and then Avi spoke, his voice surprisingly quiet: "Well, you haven't done much of anything in three months. So you're not going to get much done in five or six weeks, right?"

"Well, no, not necessarily," Des blurted.

"No, you're not," Avi cut him off with certainty. There was a pause, and they all held their breath, waiting.

"Well, I'll probably regret this," Avi continued after what seemed an eternity, "but I'll give you 'till the end of the quarter; three months."

"Thank you!" Des said enthusiastically, exhaling in relief because the extra time was even more than they had agreed to ask him for.

"But," Avi added, "I absolutely expect to see a working prototype in my hands by then."

"Absolutely, you will," Des responded. "We're all committed to that." He glanced around the table at his team, trying to mentally will them to be as determined about it as he was.

But Spec was now holding his fingers pressed to his temples, his eyes closed; Janet's face had a there's-that-"we"-word-again look; and Matt's head was buried—as usual—in his cell phone. Only Karl looked him in the eye, as if trying to size him up, wondering whether or not Des really had what it took to make good on this promise.

"We really appreciate it, Avi, thank you," Des added.

"Yeah, well . . . just get it done. Goodbye."

Des hung up and sighed again, relieved. *So, I've bought us some time*, he thought. *Not much, but some.* And he was determined to honor his commitment; no matter what it took, no matter whose butt he had to kick. In fact, while he was driving home just ten hours before, Des had made up his mind that if anyone on this team didn't step up, then he or she would be gone in a heartbeat. *This is business*, Des had reminded himself, feeling a little like he was channeling Chuck Morton; *just the way it is.*

"Des?" Karl's voice brought him back to the room.

"Yes?" he replied, looking at him.

"I'm sorry you felt that you had to lie to our customer."

"Wait a minute," Des said defensively, "you guys were the ones who said it had to be me talking to him. So I said what had to be said, and I bought us some time."

"Yes, you did," Karl said, and went quiet.

⌘

COR-Med's leadership team spent the rest of the morning struggling to hash out a strategy, not only on how to finish the Emperor prototype, but also how to reduce expenses, reorganize resources, and bring in new revenues.

Spec kept insisting that only more engineers would solve R&D's problem, while Janet kept countering that the hiring freeze had completely tied their hands. Des explained that Chuck had made it clear to him that they had to show real progress before he'd pony up more money. One thing they could agree on was that they were in a classic Catch-22 situation, although Spec had to explain to Matt what that literary reference actually meant.

Then Janet reminded them that the hiring freeze also prevented them from bringing in a new marketing director to pump life into their campaigns, and that the allegedly "brilliant" idea of having Matt wear both the head of Sales hat *and* the head of Marketing hat—as decreed by the previous CEO/CFO team—was a recipe for disaster. "No offense intended," she said, glancing Matt's way.

Understandably, this criticism prompted Matt to say "No offense taken," to put down his cell phone for once, and verbally dance around the table making reassuring noises about how he had Marketing "all under control" while waxing poetic about all the potential—yet unspecified—customers he had lined up for meetings. It was a bravura performance that distracted them enough that they decided to turn their attention elsewhere.

They briefly discussed the logic-defying fact that Manufacturing, Order Fulfillment, and Technical Support were somehow carrying on without a proper COO, chalking it up to the loyalty and doggedness of the line workers and their managers, many of whom had been with the company since its founding. But Spec contended somewhat dismissively that the line people were the least of their worries—that they'd keep at it because they desperately needed the work and had few other opportunities in a region that had seen almost all of its manufacturing and tech support jobs shipped overseas. Janet countered that COR-Med was lucky to have them and needed to try to keep them. Des agreed.

As for Karl, he assured them that the IT team, such as it was, could keep the proverbial lights on, the cloud servers secure, and their social media and web presence current, but not much more than that.

Des did his best to draw out some real action items and milestones from each of them, but it was a futile effort. They made almost zero progress, and each of them became more and more testy and irritable as the day wore on. All of their cell phones kept buzzing urgently, and it didn't help that by noon the office had started to heat up. It appeared that, once again, the air conditioning had gone on the fritz.

Finally, at around 2 p.m., they each grabbed some sandwiches that Rita had ordered and headed off to their respective offices to check messages and eat.

But Des didn't feel like eating; he was too keyed up, too worried. As far as he could tell, each of them was hunkered down in a little silo with no intention of helping the others out. On top of that, they kept sniping at each other, making cutting remarks about stuff that had happened long before he'd arrived. It was frustrating, time-consuming, and totally unhelpful.

Then, just as he was thinking about eating something—anything to change his sour mood—his cell phone rang. It was his wife, Laura. He considered not answering, letting it go to voicemail; but then he picked up, worried that something was wrong with one of his kids.

"What's up, honey?" Des answered, a little too short.

"Hey," Laura replied with a tone that said things weren't good. "I think you should know, Megan's school called. Your daughter has been skipping classes again."

"*My daughter*," he thought. "Why is it always 'my daughter' when she does something wrong?"

"Dammit! Again?!" he blurted. Defiance and skipping school were becoming recurring themes with Megan—even before their move to San Diego—along with her foul mouth and constant eye-rolling at her parents as if they were far lamer than any parents in recorded history. "Is she there now?" Des asked, thinking he could get his kid on the phone and let her have it with both barrels.

"No, she's at the mall," Laura answered.

"Why did you let her go to the mall?" Des demanded, amazed at how much of a pushover his wife could be.

"I didn't *let* her do anything!" Laura insisted. "I told her she couldn't go. But she just went anyway. She doesn't listen to me, Des. I keep telling you that."

"Well, that's not my problem. You've got to handle that with her."

"Actually, it is your problem. When she disrespects me it's both our problem."

Des knew his wife was right; as she usually was about most things. But, dammit, he didn't have time for this right now; his company was in big trouble.

"Look, I can't talk about this now. We'll deal with it when I get home tonight, OK?"

"What? At 11 o'clock again?"

He didn't appreciate her accusatory tone. "Yeah, Laura, maybe," he snapped back. "That's just the way it is right now. You know I'm in the middle of a crap-storm here. I've got a ton of angry customers and Chuck Morton breathing down my neck. And my leadership team literally hate each other."

"Yeah, Des, I know. You told me last night. But you've also got a family."

"Don't you think I know that?!" Des shouted. "What exactly do you expect me to do about Megan right now?!"

Suddenly, a very loud hammering sound—metal smashing on metal—started pounding into his office from the hallway.

"What is that banging?" his wife asked.

"I have no idea," Des snapped. "I'll call you back."

Des hung up, slammed his cell phone down on the desk, and leapt from his chair. "Rita?! What the hell is that?!"

"I think that's Grace," Rita replied from her desk in the reception area, loudly enough to be heard over the banging. "She's probably fixing something."

"Grace?" he asked, now standing in his office doorway. "Who's Grace?"

"Um, Grace, she works in maintenance. You haven't met her."

"Oh, yeah, Grace," said Des, remembering the short woman in dirty coveralls and ball cap that he'd encountered in the conference room the day before. "Yeah, I've met her. Can you tell Grace to cut it out?" he shouted. "She's driving me crazy!"

"Of course, sure," Rita got up, and made her way toward the hall. "I'll go right now."

But just then the banging stopped.

"OK, good," Des said, "I guess she heard me."

"Someone call my name?" said Grace cheerfully, now standing in the hall, carrying her red wrench, and wearing the exact same outfit she'd been in the day before. For a moment, Des thought that she hadn't gone home at all.

"Yes. We were wondering," Rita asked in a deferential tone that surprised Des, "if perhaps you could stop banging?"

"Oh, sorry about that," Grace replied to them both, coming into the reception area. "Just trying to keep the ol' girl alive."

"You can't do that another time?" Des snapped, annoyed by what he considered to be a ridiculously corny reference to a run-down building.

"I could, but you probably noticed the AC is down again."

"I noticed, believe me. It's hotter than hell in here."

"Well, I don't think it'll take me long to get it back up," Grace continued, ignoring his tone. "I just need to take off a valve, rebuild it, and put it back on."

Des was confused. "You can't just buy a new one?"

"Well, to tell ya the truth," she replied, "they don't make 'em like they used to. The new ones are made cheap; they break too easy. Now. . . ."

"So," Des responded, cutting her off, "you're saying you absolutely have to do that now."

"Well, with all the cutbacks around here, I don't think you want me doing overtime, right?" she replied. "It shouldn't take me more than an hour or two."

Des had heard enough. Throwing up his hands, he turned back into his office to grab his laptop, assuming he would have to work at home or at some coffee shop with decent Wi-Fi, just to get some peace.

But then Grace added, as if she'd read his mind, "If you're thinking of working somewhere else like a coffee shop or at home, it's probably just as noisy and distracting there."

Des stopped dead with his back toward the door. How the hell did she know that about my home, he wondered? Was she up in the ceiling, listening to my calls? This Grace person is really irritating.

Then her tone changed. "Look, Mr. Hogan, I'll try to get it done as fast as I can. I can probably do it in about 45 minutes, maybe a little more. Then you'll have your AC, nice and fresh."

Rita, playing the peacemaker, tried to bring the conversation to a close. "That would be great, Grace. Thank you very much."

But Grace had more to say. She leaned toward Des's door and called to his back: "In the meantime, Mr. Hogan, just to get away from my banging, you might want to go over to manufacturing, say 'hello' to the folks down there. I'm pretty sure they'd like to meet the new CEO."

This was too much. Des turned back to the door, grabbed it with one hand, and dismissed her with a wave of the other. "Just fix it, fast." Then he closed his door sharply on her, almost with a slam.

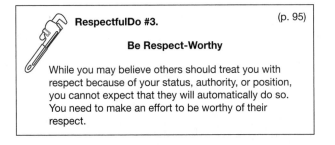

RespectfulDo #3.   (p. 95)

Be Respect-Worthy

While you may believe others should treat you with respect because of your status, authority, or position, you cannot expect that they will automatically do so. You need to make an effort to be worthy of their respect.

4

Feeling the Heat

Two weeks later, after yet another frustrating leadership meeting, it became clear to Des that things had spiraled downward even further.

Privately that morning, Janet had asked for help dealing with Spec, and Des recommended that she stop interacting with him entirely. She wasn't enthusiastic about the idea, but she'd given it a try in their meeting. The result? She said almost nothing to anyone for two hours. Not good.

As usual, Spec reported little progress on the Emperor prototype. Matt occasionally popped his head up from his phone to talk about all of the effort his sales team was putting into arranging meetings with new customers to drum up business. It would materialize, he swore, any day now. Karl claimed to be doing the opposite of Matt: keeping his head down—way down—in the electronic weeds in a frenetic attempt to keep their IT systems afloat.

As the meeting wore on, Des became more certain that very little was getting done by anyone beyond the increasing entrenchment of hostile positions. So he focused them on the balance sheet to ferret out some money they could use to hire additional engineers. But they kept hitting a brick wall, which only added to his sense of desperation. They couldn't make progress in R&D

without additional funds, and yet he didn't have the courage to tell Chuck that he was stalled. He was stuck between a rock and a hard place, to say the least, and it was driving him crazy.

Making Des's life even more complicated, the tension at home had ratcheted up quickly. His daughter, Megan, was becoming ever more defiant and rude, arguing fiercely with her mother on just about every issue and picking on her younger brother mercilessly. It had gotten so bad that there were many days when Des arrived home—usually at 8 or 9 o'clock—to find every member of his family had eaten dinner separately and retreated to their respective bedrooms as a way of avoiding conflict. Most depressingly, Des and Laura had become convinced that Megan and the boys she hung out with had started smoking cigarettes in the canyon behind the high school. On more than one occasion they got the sense that she was high, as if she'd been smoking pot, too.

But even though Des knew his family's issues were serious, he convinced himself that he had to focus all of his attention on COR-Med. Des was certain that Chuck wasn't making idle threats— that if he didn't turn things around soon, he'd lose his job, and then where would his family be? CEO positions like this don't grow on trees, he thought, and the purchase of their new San Diego home had wiped out a big chunk of their savings.

Still, his heart continued to tell him that his daughter was in trouble, so he raised the issue with Laura a few times after coming home from another exhausting and frustrating day at COR-Med. Unfortunately, their discussions always turned into tense debates about his lack of availability to his family, and ended without any plan of action other than Des saying "I'll talk to her." But as much as he wanted to, he couldn't seem to find the right time. It was a horrible feeling, so he compartmentalized it, figuring he'd deal with it when work wasn't so crazy.

To make matters even worse, just as their morning meeting ended with its usual level of tension, Chuck Morton called.

"Avi Kumar called me yesterday," his boss said tersely, dispensing with the normal greetings. "He's worried about his prototype. Really worried."

"I know, Chuck," Des said wearily. He was standing up at his desk now, with his laptop in front of him on a small platform that raised and lowered at the touch of a button. He'd read somewhere that standing desks were better for leadership energy, drive, and focus; but given the constant soreness in his feet, calves, and neck, and the lack of overall progress at COR-Med, he wasn't so sure. "We're working on it."

"What exactly is the holdup?"

"Well," Des replied, trying to sound as convincing as he could, "it's related to both software and hardware issues. I'm meeting with Spec almost every day on it."

In truth, since he had no engineering training, Des didn't quite understand the technical reasons for the holdup, other than that Spec kept saying he was going as fast as he could with the very limited resources he'd been given. Des believed him, but he didn't appreciate the accusatory language Spec spat out about just about everyone at COR-Med. And yet, to his credit, Spec did put in an awful lot of hours. Des had noticed that he was usually the first person to arrive in the morning, except for Grace, and the last to leave.

"Des, don't bullshit me," commanded Chuck. "You don't really know what the holdup is, do you?"

Dammit, thought Des. *He's too smart. I might as well just tell him the truth.* "No, Chuck, you're right. I don't specifically know what the holdup is. I'm not an engineer."

"No, you're a systems and process guy. That's why I put you there. Well, at least you can admit your limitations. That's more than I can say for the idiot you replaced."

Des thought that this was a veiled threat inside of a back-handed compliment, but at this point, he was willing to take whatever he could get.

"I appreciate that, Chuck. Listen, here's the thing about Spec and the engineers in R&D. They're a little rough around the edges, if you know what I mean. We're developing a way of working together; I think with a little more time . . . ."

"No, Des," Chuck interrupted, barking at him, "you're going to listen to me. I'm going to coach you. Here's what you're going to do. You're going to grow a spine and stand up to the geeks in your company, especially Spec. You're going to give him an ultimatum. He either comes up with a viable working prototype in the next two weeks, or he's gone. Got it?"

Des gulped. This was commanding, not coaching. Besides, he'd already been giving that very ultimatum serious consideration. But Spec really was the only one who had any idea of the entire scope of the Emperor project. Firing him meant that there was no way they would finish the prototype on time. The other engineers just weren't up to it, or so Spec claimed.

But Chuck had spoken. It was Chuck's way or the highway. "Got it," he said.

"Good!" Chuck said enthusiastically. "He'll step up if he knows his job is on the line. Now what about those other bozos over there?"

"Well, they're all trying, but they're still kind of demoralized by all the cuts and changes that, um . . . my predecessor, and his CFO made. They're still getting used to me." Since the day Des arrived, no one had ever uttered the actual names of the previous CEO or CFO. Still, they were convenient scapegoats for all of COR-Med's problems. And just about everyone on the leadership team, except for Karl, frequently blamed them for much of what was going wrong now.

"Dammit, Des!" Chuck shouted. "They don't have time to get used to you! I thought you were kicking ass and taking names! Do I have to come over there and do it myself?"

Des started to panic; the last thing he needed was Chuck descending on the place, sticking his fingers into everything and messing it all up even more than it already was. To calm Chuck down, Des decided to put on the tough guy act.

"I *am* kicking ass and taking names, believe me. Just so you know, I've called an emergency meeting with my leadership team right after lunch. They're all going to get the ultimatum, not just Spec. Trust me."

"Good. That'll shake 'em up. You need to take control of that place," Chuck replied, seemingly satisfied. "Let me know how it goes. And keep Avi Kumar happy, will ya?" He hung up without saying goodbye, as usual.

And as he had so often since the day he'd arrived, Des blew out his frustration with a loud gust of air through tightly clenched lips. OK, he thought, here we go.

RespectfulDo #4.   (p. 99)

Look for Diamonds in the Rough

It's easy to find things to criticize in other people. It's also fairly easy to find those things in others that you, and others, should respect—if you look. Look for, and acknowledge "diamonds in the rough," those things in others that are worthy of respect.

5

Commanding and Controlling

"So my point is, you all need to immediately get with the program and step up." It was a little more than two hours after Chuck's call, and Des was standing stiffly in the main conference room with his arms tightly folded, his team sitting silently around the table, staring at him. "I'm sick and tired of all of the excuses. I'm sick and tired of the delays. I'm sick and tired of all the bullshit that's going on around here." Des had deliberately decided to curse in this meeting, to let them all know how serious he was.

There was a long pause while they stared at him with surprised faces. Des had just gone further with them than ever before; he'd called them out big time on their infantile behavior and he was being more forceful than they'd ever seen. He hoped like hell it would work.

Finally, Matt spoke up, his usual slippery tone oddly missing: "So what exactly are you saying, Des?" He sounded worried, possibly even scared. Good, thought Des, I want them scared.

"I'm saying," Des continued, certain he'd struck the right tone, "that you either step up or you'll have to leave."

Spec was the first to react. "You cannot be serious!" he shouted, standing up. "What the hell do you think I've been doing all this time?!"

Matt jumped in next, leaning forward. "Hold on a second, Des. I'm doing my job, you know that. I'm not the one holding up the Emperor project."

"Oh, yeah, it's all my fault!" Spec said acidly to Matt. Then he turned back to Des, "I have stepped up. I am stepping up now. All I'm doing is stepping up all the time! And now you're threatening me?!"

Des went for the easier target first. "Actually, Matt, I don't know that you're doing your job. You say you are, but where are your results? And Spec, I am deadly serious. I'm sick of hearing about all of R&D's problems. You need to get it into overdrive immediately."

"You have got to be kidding me," Spec blurted out, dropping back down into his chair. "The only problem R&D has is sitting right over there." He looked directly at Janet, who, surprisingly, didn't react. She was staring off in the middle distance, as if her mind were somewhere else.

Then Karl spoke up: "I guess Chuck's been bugging you, huh?"

"No, he hasn't," Des lied. "This is my call. You guys just don't seem to get how serious I am. I'm telling you I've had it. Either you step up or I'll find someone who will. That's it. End of discussion."

No one said anything for a moment. They all just stared at him, in varying degrees of shock, anger, or, in Janet's case, unusual detachment.

"Unbelievable," Spec muttered under his breath to no one in particular, shaking his head.

And then Janet spoke, very softly, more softly than any of them had ever heard: "Actually, Des, I do get how serious you are."

"Good," said Des, grateful to hear that at least one of them got the message. "I'm glad."

"Well, don't be," she said, standing up slowly and deliberately collecting her cell phone and briefcase. "I'm quitting."

"What?! What did you say?!"

"I'm quitting," Janet replied, simply. She started for the door.

Des was stunned. What the hell?!

"Wait a sec!" he said, moving quickly between her and the door. "Janet, hold on, will you?" Janet stopped and stared at him coldly.

"Listen, I don't want you to quit, that's not what I want," he said, almost desperately. "You can't quit. We need you." His tone was pleading, the complete opposite of how it had sounded just moments before.

"Really?" she said. "You need me? They don't think that." With a tip of her head, she indicated the others seated at the table. Matt and Karl were staring at her, wide-eyed. Spec turned his gaze away. For a moment everything seemed to stop and no one said anything.

"Actually I do, Janet," said Karl finally, looking and sounding sincere. "We really do need you."

Janet turned back to the room, "I apologize, Karl. I know you mean that. But it's too little, too late. I know when it's time to go." Then she looked back at Des, her eyes piercing and narrow. "You'll be hearing from my lawyer."

Des was stunned. "What? You're suing us?" he stammered. "What for?!"

"Constructive discharge."

"What's that?" blurted Matt.

Janet rolled her eyes. "It means treating someone so bad that all they can do is quit. It's illegal."

Spec guffawed. "Yeah, right."

Janet turned to look directly at Spec. "And in your case, I'm suing for sexual harassment, hostile work environment, and retaliation." For a micro-second, Spec appeared to be genuinely surprised. Then he huffed, shook his head dismissively, and looked away.

"Good luck, guys." she said bluntly, heading off again. "You're definitely gonna need it." Then she stopped at the door and flashed them the same confused look she'd given Des on his very first day. "You know, Des, I just don't get the point of treating people like crap." And then she walked out.

For a moment, no one said a word. Then Des, the wind completely knocked out of his sails, shook his head in a failed attempt to clear it and slowly leaned onto the table with both hands, the intensity of the situation hitting him hard, like a baseball bat to the stomach. "Wow," he said. "Wow."

After a moment, Spec offered his two cents: "We're better off without her."

Suddenly Matt exploded up and out of his chair, yelling at Spec. "Really, dude?! Really?!! You can be a total douche bag sometimes, you know that?!"

"Yeah," Spec shot back. "I know that! But that's because I care about what happens to this company."

"As if the rest of us don't?! Jeez, you jerk!" Then Matt bolted for the door, glancing at Des on his way. "I'm going to try to talk her out of it."

"Don't bother," Spec called after him. "She wasn't helping."

They heard Matt mutter an expletive describing Spec, and then head off.

Des looked at Spec icily, and decided his head of R&D—no matter how brilliant an engineer he was—needed to be cut down to size. "Neither are you," he said, bluntly.

Spec's eyes widened for a moment then squeezed down to slits as he nodded his head arrogantly. "OK, boss," he said coolly, his lower jaw jutting out, "say the word and I'll go, too."

This was too much for Des and he leaned over the table at him, pointing his finger and shouting: "Don't push me, Spec! Don't even try it!"

"Oh, please!" Spec stood up, towering over Des. "You need me more than anyone around here. And you know that!"

"Not as much as you think! I'm telling you, don't push me!" Des was surprised by his own sudden surge of emotion. A minute before he'd been completely deflated by Janet's announcement. Now he was full of rage, out of control. He knew it, but couldn't do anything about it.

"You're not going to do a damn thing!" Spec countered confidently.

"Guys, guys, please. . ." Karl interjected, standing up and putting his hands out between them. "Everyone just calm down."

"Don't tell me to calm down!" shouted Des.

"Fine!" Karl snapped, pulling back from them both. "You just keep yelling at each other; that'll solve everything."

Spec huffed again, turned and walked to the door. "Just find us a new recruiter, will ya?" he shot back over his shoulder as he exited the room.

Des was speechless. Maybe I should fire him now, he thought. He more than deserves it. But what about Emperor?! Dammit!!

After a moment, Karl spoke up quietly, almost as if talking to himself. "You know what?" Karl said, looking at no one in particular.

"What?!" snapped Des, still in a knot.

"No one respects anyone around here."

Des couldn't disagree, so he said nothing.

"Excuse me," Karl went on. "I'll also be in my office . . . if you need me."

Alone, Des slowly sank down into a chair, and catastrophized. Losing Janet was not good. Despite her run-ins with Spec, Des had quickly come to believe that she had a sharp mind and could really have helped him turn the company around. Her threat to sue them was definitely not good. Chuck Morton could be counted on to blow a gasket. His mind raced with some disturbing images of a very possible future: Chuck's angry face up close to his, firing him; Rita quietly cleaning out his desk, putting his stuff in a cardboard box; him sitting alone at his kitchen table, unemployed, his family nowhere in sight. A feeling of deep dread came over him.

Then, with vehemence so strong that he surprised even himself, he smashed his fist repeatedly onto the conference room table and spouted a volley of curses so loudly and so foul that even a Wall Street stock trader would have blushed to have heard it.

Suddenly, he heard Grace's voice. "Is that really necessary?" It was coming from the utility closet.

Des flew out of his chair in a fury and stormed over to confront her. "Why are you spying on me, and who do you think you are talking to me like that?!"

Grace was kneeling on the utility closet floor with the red pipe wrench in her hand. She looked up at him: "I'm not spying, I'm working. And who do *you* think you are, talking to *me* like that?"

"I'm your boss, dammit!"

"So?" she said simply. "That doesn't give you the right to disrespect me." She put the wrench down, stood up, put her hands on her hips, and stared up at him with a quiet intensity.

"You've got a hell of a nerve!" Des barked.

"No," she replied, quietly but firmly. "What I've got is respect for myself. And I'm not going to let anyone disrespect me, not even you. You want to fire me, fine. Go ahead. I can always find another job, or maybe I'll retire. But you will not disrespect me."

Des shook his head, completely confused. "You're crazy, you know that?" was all he could muster.

"And you're not listening," Grace went on. "Try a little respect next time. You might get some in return. Now, if you'll excuse me."

She turned back to the closet, bent down to the floor, and started gathering up her gear into an old canvas tool bag. Instead of turning away, all Des could do was stand there and watch her in disbelief.

"You know, Mr. Hogan," she said in a matter-of-fact tone, looking back over her shoulder, "it used to be different here. Before we got bought out a couple of years ago, people used to respect each other. The company was doing just fine. Nobody was making millions as far as I know. But everybody was doing just fine. Now it's all about cutbacks, layoffs, forcing everyone who's left to do more with less, work faster or leaner or whatever the latest flavor-of-the-month management baloney it is you want to call it."

Her tools packed away, Grace stood up, turned back to Des, and looked at him intently. "But what bothers me most is that before we got bought out, no one ever, and I mean *ever*, raised their voices in anger or cursed at each other."

Des didn't have the patience to consider the value of her walk down memory lane. "Well, that's just great, Grace," he said with a hint of sarcasm. "I'm happy for you. But you don't seem to get it. This company is in real trouble; I've got to turn it around fast; I don't have time for warm and fuzzies and singing 'Kumbaya.'"

"OK, Mr. Hogan, I get it."

"Good," Des replied with finality, and started to turn away.

But Grace wasn't done. "So, Mr. Hogan, one question."

Des stopped with an annoyed sigh and turned back to her: "What's that?" he snapped.

"How's that 'tough guy' strategy working for you?"

Des immediately started to say something defensive, but after taking a long breath, he changed his mind, said nothing, and simply stared at her, thinking it through.

He had to admit, she had a point. His "step-up-or-get-out" ultimatum had completely blown up in his face. A very important member of his team had just quit and everyone remaining was madder than a bear caught in a leg trap. For the first time in a very long time, Des Hogan was at a loss for words.

Grace resettled her cap on her head, picked up her bag, and headed for the door. "Now, if you'll excuse me, Mr. Hogan, I've got work to do. Looks like you do, too."

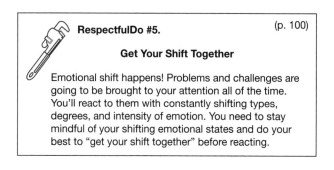

RespectfulDo #5.   (p. 100)

Get Your Shift Together

Emotional shift happens! Problems and challenges are going to be brought to your attention all of the time. You'll react to them with constantly shifting types, degrees, and intensity of emotion. You need to stay mindful of your shifting emotional states and do your best to "get your shift together" before reacting.

6

Seeing Respect in Action

Stunned by the unexpected events of the morning, Des, uncharacteristically, decided to take a walk around the block to try to clear his head and think.

As he headed out the main door, he desperately hoped he'd bump into Janet coming back into the building, having changed her mind about quitting and willing to give them all another chance. But no such luck. Neither Janet nor Matt was anywhere to be seen.

So Des walked, and walked, and walked some more, for over an hour; replaying what had happened over and over in his head. The moment Janet resigned was incredibly painful, especially since he hadn't seen it coming. He felt like a block of old granite, thick, dumb, and clueless, and he wasn't sure what he should do about her threat or who he should call for guidance.

He was, however, sure that he couldn't tell Chuck about it right away. He just didn't have the stomach for his boss's invective. In fact, given the way the plan fell apart so disastrously, he'd realized that he'd lost all respect for Chuck, and was fairly certain he was never going to trust his counsel ever again.

Finally, as he rounded the corner to go back into the building, Des concluded that Grace was right: he had work to do, serious work. His gut instincts told him that whatever he was going to do, he needed to do it fast. But what? What could he possibly do to start to turn this whole insanely crappy situation around?

As he passed the doorway to the now empty conference room, he paused to look at the utility closet and focused on his conversation with Grace. What did she say? "Try a little respect and you may get some in return." Huh. How could he do that? And with whom?

Suddenly, Des remembered a recommendation that Grace had made to him two weeks before. It's a start, he thought. It's a start!

⌘

A few minutes later, Des stepped through a cutout in a large warehouse door at the back of the main building and onto COR-Med's cavernous manufacturing floor. He instantly realized that this was the first time he'd been in this space since he'd taken over the company and then mentally beat himself up for waiting so long. That was a mistake, he thought.

He found himself looking at about a dozen different brightly lit work stations, each staffed with two to three employees in matching coveralls, smocks, and safety goggles. They were hunched over, assembling COR-Med products. Beside them stood racks of components and modules. There didn't seem to be any particular urgency to their efforts, but as far as Des could tell, they weren't slacking off either.

Off in the distance, at the back of the room, Des could see the frosted glass windows of the R&D department, Spec's domain. Ugh, Spec, he thought, big problem there. But thank goodness the employees don't know about Janet yet. He'd heard she was well liked by just about everyone—except Spec, of course—and her resignation would probably come as a big shock. Or maybe not? Maybe everyone was feeling so unhappy and disrespected that they'd figure her decision to leave—and sue!—were things that were bound to happen sooner or later. Unnerved by this possibility, he tried to put it out of his mind and stay focused on what he was there to do.

After scanning the room, he got the sense that the place was clean and tidy, and that the machinery and assembly equipment, although not exactly brand new, appeared to be fully operational. Des wondered if Grace had had anything to do with that.

After about a minute, someone somewhere let out a loud whistle, and everyone stopped what they were doing and looked toward the door in which Des was standing. Most stared at him with a look of surprise; others reached to shut off their equipment. After a moment, the room grew eerily quiet.

Des cleared his throat and made his way a bit farther in. "Hello, everyone," he said to no one in particular. "I just wanted to introduce myself. I'm Des Hogan, the new CEO."

No one replied, but one by one the employees started to walk toward him purposefully, as if they felt compelled. Soon, they were all around him in a half circle. It seemed, however, that they were wary of getting too close, and stood at a sturdy distance.

Des noticed that the group was surprisingly diverse. Given this was Southern California, he'd expected to see quite a few Latinos of both genders, but he also saw Asians, whites, and African Americans of all ages. Some appeared to be barely out of high school. Others were as old as Grace, or even older. They all stood looking at him expectantly.

Not knowing what to say, Des repeated himself: "I'm here to introduce myself. I'm Des Hogan, the new CEO."

After a long, uncomfortable pause, a youngish man with a thin, brown moustache spoke up. "Real nice of you to come by," he said, with obvious sarcasm. "The other guy never even bothered."

"Yeah, well . . .," Des retorted, looking around, "I'm not him."

"So what's going on?" continued the man, "More layoffs? If that's it, I'll say one thing for ya; at least you've got the guts to tell us to our face."

Suddenly, out of nowhere, Grace appeared at the man's side and put her hand on his shoulder. "Josh," she said casually, "I could use your help over here." Josh turned to her and Grace indicated, by tipping her head toward a corner, that they should step away from the group. Surprisingly, he complied, and they walked away, out of earshot. Thank goodness for Grace, Des thought.

Then it occurred to Des that, given the gruesome cutbacks and layoffs his predecessor had initiated, it was likely these employees would be pretty gun-shy. And he figured that if he didn't say something reassuring right away, he might soon be dealing with many more Janets walking out the door.

"Actually," he said, trying to sound as honest and as straightforward as he could, "I've decided that for now, there won't be any more layoffs." He immediately wondered from where inside his head that promise had come. He hadn't come to say that, but it popped out anyway. Fortunately, it was true. While he was desperate to find ways of freeing up money, he'd already decided that laying off even more people would severely hurt their business once he'd turned the place around and ramped up production.

The employees must have sensed his sincerity because almost all of their faces immediately softened and brightened. He also heard a couple of audible sighs of relief. Clearly, they'd been worried about their jobs, and this was welcome news.

Des was relieved as well. He desperately needed some positive responses to his leadership. So, feeling emboldened, he continued: "I know it's been rough on everyone for a while. All I'm asking is that you hang in there for a little longer while we work through some, ummm . . . stuff. I want you to know that I respect you and the work you're doing for us and I really appreciate your, uh . . . patience." That wasn't particularly well said, Des thought. But he realized that he'd meant every word and figured that it had to count for something.

It did. Des's remarks immediately provoked a number of head nods from the group, indicating that they'd understood and would do as he'd asked. Some of them even smiled, and he could have sworn that he heard one person murmur "thank you."

"OK, then . . ." Des said after a somewhat embarrassing moment of silence, "I'll let you get back to work."

"Excuse me." It was Josh, coming back from his sidebar with Grace.

"Yes?" Des said warily, not sure what was coming.

"I just wanted to apologize, Mr. Hogan," Josh said, loudly enough so everyone could hear. "I was disrespectful to you. It was hurtful. No excuses. I'm sorry about that. It won't happen again." He seemed genuinely contrite.

"Oh, heck no," Des replied, relaxing. It was the fullest, yet simplest, apology he'd ever heard. "It's OK. I completely understand. We've all been under a lot of pressure. No worries."

Josh stepped forward and held out his hand. "Thank you for coming down, sir. I'm Josh. Nice to meet you."

Des reached out and shook Josh's hand. "Nice to meet you, too, Josh."

And then, much to Des's surprise, after Josh had stepped aside, one by one the employees came up to him, looked him in the eye, told him their names, called him "Sir" or "Mr. Hogan," and shook his hand.

RespectfulDo #6. (p. 101)

Nip Disrespect in the Bud, Respectfully

Step in and nip disrespectful behavior in the bud. This usually means taking people who have been disrespectful aside and respectfully informing them that their behavior is unacceptable, that they need to fully apologize for it and not engage in it again.

7

Trying a Different Strategy

"What the hell do you mean, 'she quit'?!" Chuck shouted over the phone the morning after Des had reported the resignation to Arellus' corporate counsel.

"Exactly as it sounds, Chuck," Des replied in a just-the-facts tone of voice. "She quit, threatened to sue us, and left the building."

"That's ridiculous!" Chuck bellowed. "She's got no grounds. She's a wimp—can't hang with the big boys. I should have fired her, too!"

Des had prepared himself for Chuck's outrage and had no intention of matching it. He didn't want to rehash the incident; he just wanted to move forward.

"Well, I guess we'll see what happens with that soon enough," Des said. "In the meantime, I need to keep going. So I reached out to a headhunter I know. He's found me a potential candidate for her slot who might be perfect for us. I'm meeting with her tomorrow morning."

"Another woman? Seriously?"

"Yes, boss, another woman," said Des, definitively. "I'm going to hire the best candidate for the job. And respectfully, I'd like to ask you to let me get on with turning this company around, as I promised you I would."

"Fine. You do that," Chuck said in a less than enthusiastic tone. "But what about Emperor's prototype?"

Des took a deep breath. He'd expected Chuck was going to ask. "I'm not going to lie to you; Janet's resignation makes things more complicated. But, if I can get this new recruiter in right away, and they can bring in some new engineering talent with the skills that we need, I think we can make serious headway on it pretty quickly."

"How are you going to afford the new engineers?" demanded Chuck.

"By taking it out of my own salary."

Des could tell by the silence that Chuck was surprised by this news. But he recovered quickly. "OK. It's your money. I hope you know what you're doing."

"I hope so, too, Chuck."

Chuck hung up.

⌘

Two weeks later, Des gave their new chief talent officer, Kathleen, a tour of the facility. After introducing her to the front office staff, he made a beeline for maintenance, looking for Grace and planning to say complimentary things about her in front of Kathleen. But Grace was making a repair somewhere else in the building.

So, after introducing Kathleen to some of the employees in manufacturing—including Josh, who was very polite—he led her, with some trepidation, to R&D. As they came through the frosted door, they spotted Spec huddled with a number of engineers over a drafting table. Even though Des had alerted Spec earlier that morning that he'd be coming by with Kathleen, the head of R&D barely glanced in their direction.

After a moment's pause, they made their way toward Spec and his engineers to make the introductions. With almost zero enthusiasm, Spec shook her hand, looked her up and down, and said acridly, "I hope you can do better than the last girl we had. She was pretty worthless."

This was the kind of typically disrespectful public remark Des had come to expect from Spec, but this time he felt better prepared to hold him accountable for it. Having learned from Grace's example, Des decided not to call Spec out for it in front of his team. So, to change the topic, Des started to make a joke about the Padres' perpetually poor performance. Before he could get a word out, Kathleen cracked a wide smile and replied in an enthusiastic and genuine tone: "So you're the master engineer everyone's been telling me about! Great to meet you, Spec!" It was the perfect antidote. Spec deflated like a popped balloon.

Then, without giving him the opportunity to make another snarky remark, she turned to James Soong, Spec's longtime lead engineer, held out her hand for a firm shake, and asked him to brief her on the Emperor prototype.

Des saw his opportunity, and put his hand on Spec's shoulder. "Spec, can you help me out with something?" Spec flashed Des a quizzical look, but Des smiled casually and indicated with his head that they should step into Spec's office.

Once inside, Des sat down and asked Spec to do the same.

"What's up?" Spec asked with feigned disinterest.

Des dove right in. "Spec, you've repeatedly said how much you care about this company and how you want it to succeed."

"I do, absolutely," Spec retorted, smugly.

"And I believe you. In fact, believe it or not, we both want this company to succeed."

"So? What's your point?"

"I just heard you talk disparagingly about a former employee and disrespectfully to a new one. You did these things in front of other employees. How exactly does that behavior demonstrate you caring for this company and wanting it to succeed? Explain that to me."

Spec shrugged. "I don't have to explain myself to you or anyone."

"Actually, you do, Spec. Whether you like it or not, whether you respect me or not, you work for me."

Des could tell by the way Spec leaned forward in his chair that he was getting ready to launch into his 'I dare you to fire me' speech. And even though Des had rehearsed this moment repeatedly over the entire weekend, his heart started beating a lot faster.

He pulled a piece of paper out of his shirt pocket and held it up. "This," Des continued, trying to appear calm and confident, "is a letter terminating your employment. I haven't signed it yet. But I will if I need to, to protect the company we both want to see succeed." Spec remained frozen for a moment, apparently trying to make sense of what was happening. Then he slowly leaned back in his chair, staring at Des the whole time, and waited.

Des took a deep breath. He knew he was about to go way out on a legal limb. Arellus' corporate counsel had warned him not to say things that might come back to haunt him if he had to terminate Spec. But Des was convinced that taking this big risk was the first step in finally turning COR-Med around. It all hinges, he thought, on my ability to stay calm and focused on my goals: to keep Spec on board and engaged while completely shutting down his disrespectful behavior.

With as much deliberation as he could muster, Des reminded Spec that shortly after he had been hired as head of R&D, he'd acknowledged with his signature that he'd been trained on and understood COR-Med's sexual harassment and discrimination policy. He then reminded Spec that he'd repeated this training, as required by California law, every two years since then. Spec said nothing.

Next, Des brought up that COR-Med's policy contained the phrase "Failing to comply may result in disciplinary measures . . . up to and including termination." Spec merely did his usual dismissive huff at hearing this.

Finally, paraphrasing from his conversation with Arellus' corporate counsel, Des explained that if COR-Med terminated Spec's employment for breaching that policy—which, after an investigation, it would have every right to do—then Spec was on his own, that he might have to pay for his own legal defense if anyone—such as Janet—sued him for sexual harassment and retaliation. He added, more confident now that he'd gotten through the legal part of his speech, that in the great state of California juries typically sided with plaintiffs in harassment cases and commonly awarded damages in the six- or seven-figure range, all of which could come out of Spec's own pocket.

Now, Des knew that every bit of what he was saying could be interpreted as a threat, but he did his best to make it sound like factual information that might be of practical use to Spec, as if he were just trying to be helpful.

The look on Spec's face made it clear that he was completely surprised by what he was hearing—that he had never really considered the impact of his disrespectful behavior on others, nor the possibility that he might be held personally responsible for it.

Thrown off his game, Spec averted his eyes, leaned forward, and began to fidget with a mini-motor assembly on his desk. Finally, he cleared his throat and started to defend himself. "Look, Des, all I'm trying to do is get people to do their fricking jobs. Janet wasn't doing her job!"

"That's your opinion," Des countered. "It's not necessarily the 'truth.' And you can't possibly sit there and deny that you treated her disrespectfully in front of witnesses and that you accused her of being incompetent every chance you had."

"But she was incompetent!" Spec insisted angrily. "She never showed me any respect, and she never did anything to earn my respect."

"Again, that's your opinion," Des shot back, still staying fairly calm despite Spec's intensity. "And you never showed her any respect yourself, right? So, by your logic, you didn't earn hers either, right?" Spec, still fiddling with the motor, shrugged as if he didn't particularly care.

"But," Des went on after deliberately taking a deep breath, "that's a discussion for another time, perhaps with your attorney. Right now, you have a choice to make."

"What's that?" Spec asked.

"You can go out there and make a full apology to Kathleen for being disrespectful. . . ."

"Or. . .?"

"Or you can just sit here insisting that Janet was incompetent and unworthy of your respect, and we'll see how that plays out." Des gently fanned himself with the folded paper in his hand.

"Are you saying you'd fire me right now, without doing an investigation?" Spec countered, almost taunting him.

"That's one way it could play out," said Des. "And you could certainly sue us for wrongful termination if we did that." Des knew Arellus' attorney didn't want him to put ideas in Spec's head, but he figured he'd already said plenty that could get him in trouble, so there was no point in holding back.

"So, here's the thing," Des continued. "Our attorneys are totally confident that with your behavior, we'll easily prevail against you and recover the cost of our defense directly . . . from *you*, which he estimated would also be in the six-figure range." At this point Des started counting on his fingers. "So if you keep on being disrespectful, you're looking at having no job, being sued, losing at trial, and shelling out about a half-million dollars or more out of your own pocket. I'm pretty sure you don't want those things to happen."

Spec put down the motor carefully, leaned in, and pulled out what he thought was his ace in the hole. "If you fire me," he warned, "Avi Kumar will never get his prototype. And Chuck will toss you out on your ass just as fast as he did the last guy."

But Des had prepared for this threat as well. "Spec, why do you think Kathleen is out there right now talking to James Soong and the rest of the engineers about the Emperor prototype?" Spec peered at him, trying to parse where this was going.

"You don't need to answer that," Des continued. "I'll tell you why. Because I've already asked her if she knows of any hot engineers we could poach from one of our competitors who actually could get that thing done. She assured me that she did know one or two, and I believe her. Spec, you're a totally brilliant engineer; that's one of your diamonds in the rough. And you are very rough, trust me. No doubt about it, we owe a lot of our success to you; and I respect you for it. But we're going to get Avi his prototype with or without you; I guarantee it."

Spec shook his head dismissively: "You don't have the money to hire new engineers."

"I do if I take it out of my own salary," Des replied calmly.

"You won't do that."

"Wanna bet?"

Spec started to respond, but then paused. He stared hard at Des and tried to appear unfazed by the whole conversation. But, after a moment, his eyes started to twitch. It looked to Des like Spec was finally waking up to the fact that he wasn't indispensable, that the company he professed to care so much about could actually be successful without him.

Then Spec took off his glasses, rubbed his eyes, and turned his gaze away. After what seemed like an eternity of looking around his office and up at the ceiling, he sighed, put his glasses back on, and looked directly at Des. "So what exactly do you mean by 'full apology'?"

RespectfulDo #7. (p. 104)

Offer a Full Apology for Disrespect

One of the hardest things for a leader to do is apologize. This is because leaders are afraid of appearing to be weak. Yet, there's plenty of evidence demonstrating that leaders who do offer genuine, full apologies are more respected by their employees afterward.

8 | Causing Alarm

After some coaching from Des, Spec's full, public apology to Kathleen was fumbling and inarticulate. But, to his credit—or maybe because he was smart enough to know he was really boxed in—he tried his best to be sincere, and Kathleen accepted it, quickly and graciously. While Spec was apologizing, Des noticed that James Soong and the other engineers were so surprised by what Spec was doing that he was convinced he could have knocked them all over with a feather.

⌘

Three weeks later, as promised, Kathleen had brought on board two hot-shot engineers, one of whom Spec knew from their time together as graduate students at Stanford. Although their salaries and signing bonuses ate up a very substantial portion of Des's salary, he was convinced that hiring them was his only option. He'd also discussed it with Laura, who gulped hard when she heard the idea. But she told him that if he felt it was the right thing to do she would support him.

The two engineers set to work immediately on the Emperor prototype, and after a week, for the first time in a long time, Spec reported that they had started to make some, albeit slow, progress.

Unfortunately, as a result of Janet's resignation and threatened lawsuit and the plodding pace of R&D, Chuck went back on his promise to let Des turn the company around on his own. Despite Des's strong objections, Chuck insisted on daily update emails from Des and weekly conference calls with the COR-Med leadership team.

Des felt extraordinarily disrespected and undermined by Chuck's demands, but he bit the bullet and refocused his energy on his leadership team. Together, they kept trying to reassure Chuck that everything was OK. Kathleen proved to be particularly adept at soothing his troubled waters. But Matt seemed stuck; he had little to report in terms of winning major customers. And Karl kept cutting back wherever he could, which was almost nowhere since he'd already cut IT to the bone.

Within a few weeks the truth had become obvious to all: expenses were holding steady—or increasing—while revenues were lagging. There was no question any more: COR-Med's fortunes were tied directly to their success in satisfying their biggest customer, Emperor Health Care.

One morning, about seven weeks out from Avi Kumar's deadline, they had a particularly frustrating leadership meeting in the conference room. Spec reported a major technical hiccup with the prototype; and Karl admitted what he'd suspected for some time, that their customer databases had been hacked. While they were trying to digest these two pieces of bitter news, Des started getting distracting texts from his wife and his daughter, both sending him the same message: "Call me." Des had simply replied "Wait."

Although they weren't able to help Spec, the leadership team started wordsmithing with Karl on an announcement to their customers, apologizing for the data breach and reassuring them that all would be well soon. It was humbling work.

Then, just as they began to debate the best date to announce the breach, Des's cell phone rang. It was his daughter, Megan. Wow, he thought, she never calls me at work. Something must really be wrong. Des abruptly excused himself from the meeting, stepped into the hallway, and answered.

"Dad!" she insisted. Des could tell she was very angry. "Dad, I need to talk to you about Mom!"

Oh God, he thought; not now. He turned his back to the conference room door and walked a few paces down the hall, hoping his team couldn't hear. "Megan," he said with a hushed tone of annoyance, "can't this wait till I get home tonight?"

"No. I need to talk to you now. Mom is being a total bitch to me."

Whoa! Megan had never called her mother that word before. His shock almost immediately turned to fury. "Wait a minute," he barked. "Don't you ever, ever call your mother that word. Ever!"

"But, Dad . . . ."

"I don't care what you think she's done to you; you will never ever call her that word again! You will not disrespect your mother! Do you understand me?!" He knew he'd begun to shout, but he felt like he had to just to get through to her, her offense was so huge.

"You're just like she is!" Megan shouted back at him. He could tell she was starting to cry, but he didn't care. He had to drive home his point.

"Actually, I can be a hell of a lot meaner than she is!" he shouted. "And the only bitch in this family is you!!"

Megan hung up. He pulled the phone from his ear and stared wide-eyed at it, unable to fathom how she could be so disrespectful, not only to her mother but also to him. He just couldn't believe how much his daughter was driving him crazy. Does raising a kid really have to be this difficult, he wondered.

After shaking his head in a futile attempt to clear it, Des decided he just didn't have the time to deal with personal distractions like these and strode back into the conference room, where he came face-to-face with Chuck Morton, standing at the head of the table.

"Chuck," Des blurted out with obvious annoyance, "What are you doing here?!"

"Well," Chuck replied sarcastically, "nice to see you, too."
Then Des noticed that his entire team was staring at him, their eyes
open far wider than he'd ever seen.

OK, Des thought, this is just freakin' great. First, my daughter
calls her mother the B-word and hangs up on me; then Chuck
shows up out of the blue; and now my entire leadership team is
looking at me like I've got two heads. It was all too much for Des,
and he lost it completely.

"Dammit, Chuck," he said, getting up in the bigger man's
face. "I can't believe you have the nerve to come here. But I'm
glad you are. Because I've been meaning to tell you . . . you have
screwed everything up!"

"I've screwed everything up?!" Chuck fired back, incredulously.
"I have?!"

"Yeah, you! You told me you'd let me get on with turning
this place around. But instead you just keep sticking your nose into
my business. You're a freakin' bully! You know that?!"

"What?!"

"You need to get the hell out of my building right now!"

"Your building?!" Chuck countered, his face now bright
red. "Your building?! This is *my* building. And this is my
company and I could fire you right now and shut this place
down if I wanted to, and then it definitely won't be your
building anymore."

Des went all in. "Well, then maybe that's what you should
do!" he said bitterly. "It's falling apart anyway! You can have it."

"Des, please . . . ." It was Kathleen, trying to intervene carefully. "Maybe we should all take a break."

"No, Kathleen," Des snapped rudely, still staring at his boss.
"Chuck, I am sick and tired of being disrespected by you, and
second-guessed, and micro-managed, and ordered around like I'm
some kind of child. I'm done with it."

"So you're done with it?!" Chuck demanded.

"Yup, I'm done with it. Do I need to say it again?"

"Nope," said Chuck with finality. "OK, then. Have it your way. . . ." And just as he was about to do his best Donald Trump impersonation and say "You're fired!" the fire alarm went off.

During the late 1990s, the state of California—notorious for its many wildfires and earthquakes—updated its building and renovation codes, requiring all commercial facilities to install what are commonly known as "Whooping and Rising X3" types of alarms. Anyone who's ever been in a building when these kinds of alarms are sounding knows that they are shockingly loud, and they can drown out anything someone says or shouts, even when standing face-to-face.

So no one in that conference room, not even Des, heard Chuck terminate his employment. Instead, they were all so startled and so deafened by the alarm that they instinctively leapt from their seats, grabbed their gear, and dashed out into the hallway where, much to their surprise, the alarm was even louder.

Within the span of 15 seconds, the members of COR-Med's leadership team and the CEO of their parent company found themselves out in the building's main parking lot, squinting under the bright, hot Southern California sun and poking their fingers into their ears as if trying to literally pry out the piercing sound of the alarm.

All that most of them could say was, "Oh, my God, that was loud!" or "Holy crap!" followed by some pained replies in agreement.

But Des had a different reaction. The alarm had instantly dispelled his rage, and by the time they'd gotten outside, he'd become desperately concerned that his building was burning down and that there could be employees trapped inside.

"Stay out here!" he shouted in a powerful, commanding voice that he had no idea he possessed. "I'm going to get everyone out!"

Des had sprinted more than halfway up the walkway to the front entrance by the time Matt shouted, "Wait for the fire department!" and was into the building before anyone could stop him.

Forcing himself to ignore the still screaming alarm, he raced down the hallway toward the main office and checked inside, looking for Rita. No sign of her. "Rita's out!" he said out loud without hearing himself. "That's good!"

Then, as he bolted to the back of the building toward manufacturing and R&D, he realized he'd have to pass the maintenance office and could check to see if Grace was there. She'd be the kind, he thought, to stay in the building and fight the fire, to protect "the ol' girl."

Sure enough, as he rounded the corner and looked into the maintenance office, he saw that Grace was, in fact, still inside the building. But he quickly realized that she wasn't fighting any fire; she was simply standing at the wide open door of the alarm control box with her thumb pushing firmly on a big, red button marked "Test."

The moment she saw Des, Grace released the button, and the alarm stopped as suddenly as it had started.

The silence was deafening. Des was flabbergasted. "Grace! What are you doing?!" he demanded. "Why didn't you warn us that you'd be testing the alarm today?!"

"I'm not testing it," she said, somewhat dryly with a sigh. "I'm stopping you from making a big mistake."

"What?!"

"I said, 'I'm stopping you from making a big mistake.' You were about to get yourself fired and that is the last thing that this company needs."

"But," stammered Des, "you can't just . . . you can't just . . . you don't have the right to do that!"

"No, Mr. Hogan, I don't have the right to do that. But what are you going to do, fire me? Or call me the 'B-word,' like you did your daughter?"

Des was stunned. "How do *you* know I did that?!"

"Mr. Hogan, you shouted so loud the whole building knows you did it."

As Des flashed back to the end of his fight with Megan, he suddenly realized why his team was looking at him cross-eyed. His mouth dropped open with stunned embarrassment and his eyes shot to the top of the room, desperately searching for a giant bolt of lightning to strike and put him out of his misery. Then, just as suddenly, all of the energy drained from Des's body and he collapsed against the door, overwhelmed, unable to say or do anything.

Grace took his arm gently, steered him to an old, wooden office chair, and sat him in it. She produced a bottle of water, opened it for him, and said "drink." Des did as he was told and then sat mutely, trying to make sense of all that had happened in the past ten minutes. Do I still have a job, he wondered? Do I still even have a family? Grace leaned against the desk, folded her arms, and stared at him.

After a long silence, Des said quietly, "Grace, I can't believe I did that."

"What?" she asked, "Dare Chuck to fire you, or call your daughter the B-word?"

"Both," said Des, after some consideration. "I really screwed up."

"Just exactly when are you going to learn, Mr. Hogan, that trying to stop disrespect with even more disrespect is always going to make things a lot worse."

"I think I just did," Des said. "I think I learned it the hard way."

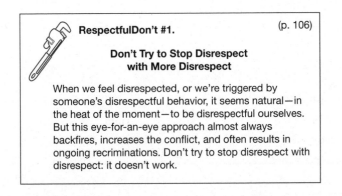

RespectfulDon't #1. (p. 106)

**Don't Try to Stop Disrespect
with More Disrespect**

When we feel disrespected, or we're triggered by someone's disrespectful behavior, it seems natural—in the heat of the moment—to be disrespectful ourselves. But this eye-for-an-eye approach almost always backfires, increases the conflict, and often results in ongoing recriminations. Don't try to stop disrespect with disrespect: it doesn't work.

9 | Apologizing

By the time Des had made his way back to the conference room, the rest of his team, along with Chuck, had already reassembled inside. They were sitting around the big table waiting for him.

Des walked in slowly, stopped, and looked around at them. "No fire," he said quietly, shaking his head. "Just a test."

"We kinda figured," said Matt.

Chuck, his face dark and his tone serious, couldn't hold himself back. "OK, Des. Before we were interrupted, I was about to. . . ."

"Chuck, I'm sorry to interrupt you again," Des said purposefully, "but I have to something to say."

"Don't you think," interjected Spec, the last person Des thought he'd hear from at a moment like this, "that you've said enough, Des? Maybe you should listen to Chuck first."

"Well, maybe I should, Spec," Des responded, with a tone that made it clear he was not going to take his advice. "But I have to get this off my chest now."

"Okaaaayyy," said Chuck. "Go ahead."

Des took a deep breath and spoke with a firmness and authenticity that none of them had ever heard from him before.

"I owe you all an apology," he stated clearly, with a sense of finality. The room grew very still. "Since the day I got here, I've been disrespectful. I've been rude, arrogant, abrupt, dismissive, distracted, condescending, and a whole lot more. In short—and this is the most accurate word I can use—I've been an asshole. I've been that way to you, too, Chuck."

"That's true," Chuck concurred, nodding gently.

"There's no question in my mind," Des continued, "that my behavior has been offensive. I have no excuses. There are no excuses for disrespect. I'm sorry."

Des paused to think. He wanted what he was about to say to come out right, and fortunately no one interrupted him, so he was able to choose his words carefully.

"I believe I have to make it up to each and every one of you. And I'm committed to doing that. But, to tell you the truth, I think I've gone too far. I honestly don't think that I can lead this company right now."

"Now, hold on a minute," Chuck interjected. "Please, Des, don't say anything more. Please." It was the word "please" that stopped Des. He'd never heard Chuck say it before, and he stared at him, puzzled.

"Look, Des," said Chuck, "everyone's been under a huge amount of pressure here. And sure, some people have behaved like jerks. You definitely did. But that's no reason for you to quit."

"I don't understand," Des said. "You were about to fire me."

"Forget about what I was about to do," Chuck said, waving his hand as if to banish the idea. "I've changed my mind. The last thing this company needs is for me to fire you."

Des was startled. "Wait, have you been talking to Grace?" he asked, wondering if she was some kind of guardian angel, looking after him.

"Who's Grace?" Chuck asked. "No, I haven't talked to any Grace. No, I've been talking to Spec and everyone else here." Des glanced over at Spec, who raised his eyebrows and tilted his head as if to say "listen to the man."

"Now you've made your apology. It was a good one and the right thing to do. Good for you. I might even try it myself . . . someday . . . maybe." Everyone on the team grinned at this, except for Des, who remained staring intently at Spec.

"Anyway," Chuck went on, "Spec just gave it to me straight, and everyone at this table agrees with him, that you're making real progress here, and that I've got to cut you—cut all of you—some slack, and let you get on with it without, as you said, me sticking my nose into it all the time."

Des was stunned. He'd told his team on a number of occasions that he believed that they were making some progress, but he hadn't heard anyone agree with much enthusiasm, least of all the head of R&D, who was generally negative about everything. He never imagined that Spec would be the one to go to bat for him with Chuck.

"So, that's what I'm going to do, you understand? Let you get on with it. In fact, I'm going call Avi Kumar and buy you a little more time, if you want it."

This offer was a bit of a surprise, and Des wasn't sure how to respond. He looked directly at Spec, who looked at the others on the team, who one by one shook their heads as if to say, "We don't need more time." Spec looked back at Des and shook his head the same way. Reassured, Des turned to Chuck: "We'll meet the deadline."

"Good. I trust you," Chuck replied.

Just at that moment, Des noticed that the conference room's air conditioning kicked in. It felt cool and refreshing, and Des made a mental note to thank Grace for it. In fact, he realized that he had a lot to thank Grace for.

"Now, Des," Chuck continued, "this is going to sound like a command, and maybe it is. But you need to go home right now and apologize to your daughter. It doesn't matter what she's done. Family is the most important thing; you know that. You need to take time off and focus on them, get things straightened out there. And these good people right here," he said, pointing around the room purposefully, "they're going hold down the fort while you're gone."

"But. . . ." Des protested.

"No 'buts' about it," Chuck retorted, looking over to Spec for confirmation.

Spec stood up slowly, leaned on the table, and looked Des right in the eye. "Des, I think what Chuck is telling you, what I'm telling you—hell, what we're all telling you—is to please shut up and go home . . . for a little while."

"At least two weeks," added Kathleen.

"Take all the time you need, Des," Matt said.

"But, what about. . .?" Des tried again.

"Des," said Karl reassuringly with a determined smile, "you have to trust us. It'll be OK."

RespectfulDon't #2.   (p. 109)

Don't Tolerate Disrespect

Disrespect has an incredibly negative impact on relationships, collaboration, productivity, and the bottom line. Don't tolerate disrespectful behavior, no matter how inconsequential it may seem. You need to hold those who behave disrespectfully accountable.

10 Turning It Around at Home

And it was. Des took two weeks off for an unplanned, but desperately needed vacation with Laura and their kids at his parents' old Victorian home in western Massachusetts. There were a lot of late night talks and late night tears while they unwound, reconnected, and focused on their future as a family. He was able to genuinely apologize to his daughter and she, in turn, sincerely apologized to her mother. Interestingly, grandma proved to be particularly adept at helping Megan and her mom to start communicating without fighting. "I've been here before," she said with a knowing smile, "with Des's sister."

However, it wasn't all Happy Valley, especially when Megan admitted to them that she'd been smoking pot and hanging out with some cigarette smokers to cover the smell. After devising her own punishment—grounding without cell phone for two months!—she asked her parents if they would consider moving to Colorado at some point in the future. Laura and Des did their best to suppress a smile at her cleverness and gently encouraged their daughter to focus on the present and not to "push it."

They also agreed on some ground rules around treating each other more respectfully. These included engaging in common courtesies like saying "good morning" and "good night" every day, and taking the time to genuinely ask how everyone was doing. They agreed to listen to each other's concerns more closely—without being on their smart phones at the same time—and to be less judgmental and dismissive.

They also instituted bans on yelling at and interrupting each other, and created a signal for a 30-second "cooling off" period when they were angry at each other, during which no one could speak, not even Laura or Des. Both of their kids insisted on this last condition, basing it on the idea that everyone needed to treat everyone else with respect and fairness, regardless of who was the parent and who was the child. "What's good for the goose," said their precocious son, with wisdom far beyond his years, "is good for the gander." How he'd heard that particular phrase, they didn't know, but the grandparents were strongly suspected. Still, in the spirit of mutual respect, Des and Laura agreed to the terms.

RespectfulDon't #3.   (p. 111)

Don't Be Distracted

We have reached a point at which our electronic devices are distracting us almost constantly, at work and at home. Everyone's doing it; and it's disrespectful, even though we don't mean it to be. And your emotional states can also be distracting (see RespectfulDo #5). Don't be distracted.

---

11 | Turning It Around at Work

Des returned to COR-Med a man on a mission. During his vacation, he'd met another CEO—someone just like him in age, temperament, and experience—who'd had very similar challenges and issues at his own company. He'd overcome them, and now his company was thriving. When Des pressed him for the secret to how he'd done it, how he'd turned everything around, the CEO replied that he had simply realized that being a total jerk, yelling and cursing at people, and giving them ultimatums just wasn't working: that he needed to treat everyone with respect regardless of who they were; that he needed to hold everyone accountable for disrespectful behavior; and that he needed, perhaps more than anything, to feel that he was behaving like a decent human being. "For me," he said, "It was all about just choosing to be respectful." He added that, because he'd changed his attitude and behaviors, not only did he feel like he'd turned everything around for the better at his company, but that his personal life—his own sense of well-being—was far better than ever before.

Des was stunned at how simple it all seemed. After considering how he could do that at COR-Med, he asked the CEO whether he'd be willing to meet again, to talk more about what he'd done and how he'd done it. Instead, the CEO gave him the name and number of a consultant and executive coach who was an expert on respect. Des immediately called the consultant and, after a brief conversation, hired them.

Together they determined that Des's first task upon his return to work was to demonstrate to everyone that he was a "changed man" when it came to the way he was going to treat others—respectfully, all of the time—followed immediately by a very open, honest, and energetic effort at repairing his professional relationship with his leadership team while instilling a culture of respect throughout the company. The consultant made it clear that it wasn't going to be easy and that it was going to take time, but Des knew himself well enough to know that, once he'd made up his mind to do something, he was like a dog with his teeth clamped firmly on a pant leg: he'd never let go.

It also became clear to Des that creating a Respectful Leadership culture wasn't going to be the cure for all of COR-Med's ills and that everything would just run smoothly after that. No, he learned that real organization development was an ongoing process and that there were other key aspects—and people—within his company that might need to change. As daunted as he was by all that needed to be done, he took heart in knowing that he was really, finally choosing to do the right things for COR-Med and for everyone who worked there. It felt good, really good.

Down in R&D, while Des was gone, Spec, James Soong, and the rest of the engineers had also significantly ramped up their efforts and gotten creative. Now that Chuck was no longer hovering over them like a Predator drone, they decided to order a dozen cases of mega-energy drinks and pull a record-breaking ten-day string of back-to-back all-nighters. About a month later, a few weeks after Des's return, they finished the prototype, four days before the deadline. Then, Des, Spec, and Matt flew up to Oakland to present it to Avi Kumar.

COR-Med's biggest customer was more impressed than anyone could have hoped. Avi declared the device "well worth the wait!" and immediately put in such an unexpectedly large order that Matt blurted out, "Holy shit, really?!," right in front of everyone. "Really," they replied, laughing. He spent the rest of the meeting apologizing profusely to them for being disrespectful. This incident—like the unexpected fire alarm that was just a "test"—soon became legendary in COR-Med history.

Fortunately, as a result of that one huge order, Matt seemed to get his sales mojo back. From then on, it was fairly common for him to excitedly whisper to Des that they'd made yet another massive sale, taking care to avoid foul language and instead calling it a "Holy Matt Sale," which was somewhat self-aggrandizing, but amusing all the same. That practice also fell into legend.

For Des's part, the Emperor order and Matt's revitalized sales success relieved him from constantly worrying about keeping the doors open. With Kathleen's help, they hired a cracker-jack CFO who was able to sort out COR-Med's accounts and help them reorganize their spending. Chuck released his grip on their budgets and gave Des an end-of-year bonus that more than made up for what he'd had to pay the new engineers.

They also brought in a new director of marketing to whom Matt was more than happy to hand the reins. He finally admitted that he'd been overwhelmed by having to wear two hats, and everyone empathized, assuring him they knew he was just trying to be a "good soldier." His replacement was a young African-American woman named Alyssa. She'd been in marketing roles in two big pharma firms for a few short years and had then gone off to earn her MBA from Boston University's Questrom business school. She immediately set her sights on refreshing the overall look and feel of the COR-Med brand. With Karl's expertise and a newly hired team of Millennials, she exponentially improved their online presence. The COR-Med brand and its products had never looked better.

With coaching from his Respectful Leadership consultant, Des began transforming his leadership behaviors. He started greeting everyone at COR-Med with a smile and "Good Morning!" or "Hello!" He regularly and sincerely acknowledged the employees, sometimes in public, not only for meeting their business goals but also for their skills and the respectful ways they treated each other. He found methods of managing his temper—starting with deep breathing and short walks outside—and by putting bad news into perspective, reminding everyone that things could be far, far worse, that they had solid, reliable people at COR-Med, and that if they came together as a team they could always work things out.

He instituted monthly "all hands" meetings in which he discussed the company's status with all employees as openly and honestly as he could. They were always well attended and well received. He also personally partnered with human resources to develop and champion what they called the "Respectful Employee Salute Program," which genuinely rewarded employees not only for meeting and exceeding their goals but also for treating everyone— including their customers, fellow employees, suppliers, vendors, and their community—with respect. Not surprisingly, people also started talking about nominating COR-Med for a coveted "Best Place to Work" Award.

Leadership meetings began to go much more smoothly after Des's return. He instituted a ban on cell phones and other distractors and a process for consistently driving their agendas forward respectfully, efficiently, and effectively. He stopped interrupting people and asked others to follow suit. No one threatened anyone anymore, and when tensions ramped up, they'd deliberately take a break, go outside into the sunlight, and then revisit their disagreements with a calmer, more reasonable attitude. He also insisted that there would be no more shouting or cursing at each other, except for the occasional "Good job!!" or "Damn, you're good!!!"

Also, against his attorney's advice, Des called Janet, who was very surprised to hear from him. He began by respectfully asking whether she had a few moments to listen to what he had to say and giving her the option to say "no." She replied that she had 60 seconds. Des then took responsibility for the disrespect she'd experienced at COR-Med, offered her a full apology, including a promise that he would never again tolerate disrespectful behavior at COR-Med by anyone. He also told her that she'd be receiving a very generous severance offer very soon. He said he hoped that she would accept his apology and the offer, and he wished her well regardless of what she decided. Janet said nothing while he spoke, but before they hung up she thanked him for reaching out and ended by saying, "I appreciate the apology."

Unfortunately, after six weeks of being on good behavior, Spec began to revert to his previous self, sniping at his team and colleagues, trashing their ideas, and popping off with foul language and angry, sarcastic tirades. It got to the point that a number of people, including Matt, Karl, Kathleen, and the new engineers, began to question Des's oft-mentioned commitment to maintaining a respectful workplace. Des found himself defending Spec to them, reminding them of how brilliant he was, and the incredible products that came out of R&D. At the same time, he surreptitiously kept taking Spec aside and pointing out to him how his behavior was hurting COR-Med. Each time Spec would offer a reluctant apology and take one painfully small step forward. But, sadly, he'd fall back into his old habits and take two steps back.

Finally, eight months after the Emperor order came in, after having authorized an internal investigation of Spec's behavior, after having the consultant coach him, and after repeatedly warning him and putting him on a formal, documented, improvement plan with very few positive results, Des realized that he was backed into a corner and had no choice but to let Spec go. He got Chuck's approval, met with their corporate counsel, assembled a fair severance package, and then quietly informed Spec of his termination in a private meeting offsite.

Even though they both knew it was coming, it was one of the most uncomfortable meetings Des had ever had, and Spec didn't make it any easier by angrily threatening to sue him and COR-Med. But Des kept his cool and quietly made it clear that if he stopped being the Respectful Leader, if he stopped holding people accountable for their disrespectful behavior—even people as technically brilliant and as valuable as Spec—then all of their hard work and success in turning COR-Med around would go down the drain. Spec declared that it was all "politically correct bullshit" and told Des he'd hear from his attorney. At the end of the meeting, which lasted only ten minutes, Des offered his hand. Spec refused to take it. Nevertheless, Des wished him the best, and it was done.

RespectfulDon't #4.   (p. 112)

Don't Minimize the Power of Respect

Too often leaders feel that respect isn't all that important, that it's touch-feely and intangible. Or they've got thoroughbreds in their stable, brilliant geniuses who may be incredibly rough on people but are tolerated because of their valuable contributions to organizational success. Leaders who feel like this are grossly underestimating and minimizing the power of respect and the destructive nature of disrespect.

12

Grace's Gift

Nearly a year to the day after the Emperor order came in, and a few months after Spec's release, Grace stood up at an all-hands meeting, took off her Padres cap, and announced that the "ol' girl" (meaning 'the building') was "in the best shape she's been in for years!" Everyone cheered. "This means," she continued, "that it's time for this 'ol' girl'—I mean me—to retire."

Everyone was surprised, especially Des, who took her aside after the meeting and practically begged her to stay. She declined, proclaiming that they didn't need her help anymore, that they'd be fine without her. Des disagreed, but respectfully accepted her resignation.

Still, Des was determined not to let her leave the company without proper acknowledgment. So he and the leadership team decided to throw Grace a retirement party, complete with hot food, generous gifts—including a ten-day river cruise for two in Europe—a big cake, and a rock band made up of COR-Med employees, including Karl, who to everyone's surprise played a mean lead guitar, and Kathleen, who sang vocals.

Everyone who worked at COR-Med, and their families, were invited to the party. Grace brought her spouse—a woman. It appeared that Des was the only employee who didn't know that

Grace was gay, and he quickly shrugged off his slightly startled reaction by saying to himself "to each his—or her—own."

On the big day, the entire warehouse area of COR-Med, which had been especially cleared out and decorated for the event, was bursting at the seams with people singing, dancing, and enjoying each other's company. Even Josh, who'd been promoted to director of operations, danced and declared it the best party he'd ever attended.

Halfway through the festivities, Des got up and said some heartfelt things about Grace and all the great things she'd done for COR-Med. There was a lot of cheering and hooting; universal agreement that Grace was unique, beloved by all, and irreplaceable. She would be really missed. Grace was genuinely embarrassed, and obviously touched.

As the party wound down, Des and Grace found themselves walking together down the hallway toward maintenance. She'd told him she needed to fetch a personal item from her office that she'd forgotten and asked if he would accompany her to get it.

When they got to the maintenance office, Grace marched over to her old canvas toolkit and began to rummage through it. "So," she said in a serious tone as she searched, "I owe you an apology, Mr. Hogan."

"What for?"

"Because," she said, her head still buried in the bag, "I lied to you."

"What?" Des said, disbelievingly. "You've never lied to me, Grace, ever."

"Well, this one time I did. See, I told you that I'd forgotten a personal item that I needed to get. That's not true. I don't forget things. I may be old," she continued with her character-istic bluntness, "but my memory is still as sharp as a brand-new X-Acto knife."

"No doubt about that," Des said, smiling at yet another of Grace's corny-but-cute references.

"No, Mr. Hogan," she continued seriously, "I lied to you because I wanted to get you in here so I could give you this." She pulled her hand out of the bag, turned around and held up a large, red pipe wrench, smeared in grease.

Des recognized it immediately: it was the one she'd dropped in the utility closet on his first day at COR–Med. He suddenly felt a lump grow in his throat and turned his head away, surprised and embarrassed by his emotions.

"Now, I'm giving you this tool," Grace continued, ignoring his discomfort, "because this belongs to the company. It's not mine. The company paid for it a long time ago, and I don't want to be accused of stealing company property."

Des attempted to clear his throat: "No, we certainly wouldn't want that."

"No, we wouldn't. So here you go." With little ceremony, she wiped the wrench off with a cloth and presented it to him.

"You know, Grace," Des said as he took it, a wry smile spreading across his face, "for a moment there, I thought you might be giving this to me as a reminder."

"Reminder of what?"

"To hit myself over the head with it whenever I don't treat people with respect."

"Oh, no, Mr. Hogan," she said with a grin and a wink, "I would never do such a disrespectful thing."

"I'm sure you wouldn't, Grace. I'm sure you wouldn't."

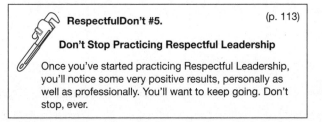

RespectfulDon't #5.   (p. 113)

Don't Stop Practicing Respectful Leadership

Once you've started practicing Respectful Leadership, you'll notice some very positive results, personally as well as professionally. You'll want to keep going. Don't stop, ever.

PART

II

Respectful Leadership

Summary and Overview

If you think about it for just a moment, you'll realize that everyone—
every single person, no matter who he or she is—wants respect.
Don't you?

People want to be treated politely, with courtesy, consideration, and genuine regard everywhere they go, in any situation. At
work, people want to be treated with common courtesy and to be
respected for their skills and experience. They want their personal
and life choices not to be judged, denigrated, or criticized. They
want to be treated fairly and honestly by their bosses; and when
they make a mistake, they want to be told about it respectfully, in
private. In short, everyone wants to be treated respectfully.

I've never met or heard of anyone who has actually wanted to
be disrespected, ignored, denigrated, micro-managed, and treated
rudely by a boss or colleagues in public or in private. Have you?
In reality, no one—and I mean no one—wants to be disrespected.

And yet, as you've probably realized from your own experience and from reading *The Respectful Leader*, disrespectful behavior
in the workplace is all too common.

You've probably heard of the management and leadership style called "Command and Control," which roughly translates into "Do as I tell you, because I'm your boss." Managers and supervisors who use the command-and-control style prefer to tell subordinates what to do and how to do it, sometimes in great detail, and then closely supervise to ensure their orders are carried out. Historians trace the emergence of command-and-control style back thousands of years to the establishment of formal military organizations in which obedience and discipline were paramount.

In the workplace, command-and-control came into common usage at the beginning of the Industrial Revolution when bosses needed to ensure accurate repetition of tasks in a short period of time in order to maintain quantity and quality. It's also a technique many people learned when they were children: "Do as I say because I'm your parent." Regardless of its origins, command and control is a very common management style that can be found in many, if not most, organizations.

A slightly subtler derivative of command-and-control is the practice of using the "carrot-and-stick" technique to drive performance. In other words, "you'll be rewarded if you do your job as commanded, and punished if you don't." Maybe you had or have had a boss who operates using the command-and-control/carrot-and-stick approach, or maybe you practice it yourself.

Here's the fundamental problem with this management style: decades of research and study, along with millions of employee surveys and mountains of anecdotal evidence from all over the world, make it abundantly clear that the vast majority of human beings who are on the receiving end of this approach simply don't like it. Most people resent being bossed around, told exactly what to do, and micro-managed by their boss. And they feel the carrot-and-stick approach is demeaning and ignores the possibility that they might actually want to do a good job out of personal pride, or because they genuinely care about doing the right thing and creating good outcomes—not just because they're being rewarded and punished.

Now don't get me wrong, I'm fully aware that command-and-control management can be a very useful and effective technique in certain types of organizations, for example, the military or emergency services. If we're in the middle of a firefight or trying to stop a house from burning down, we don't have time for a respectful discussion about how we're going to respond. Someone's got to be in charge and say, "You, do this" and "You, go there." There's nothing inherently wrong with the command-and-control style when it comes to effectively responding to life-and-death situations. But when no one's life is on the line, then most people consider it disrespectful. As we've established, no one wants to be disrespected.

Command-and-control's direct offspring, carrot and stick is also usually considered disrespectful by those subjected to it. Studies tell us that when faced with a choice between a higher wage job working for a manager who consistently uses the carrot-and-stick approach and the same job at a lower wage under a manager who practices Respectful Leadership, most employees will choose the latter if they have the option.

In the final analysis, the command-and-control/carrot-and-stick management style foments fear and stress in the workplace because it is disrespectful, demotivating, intimidating, and occasionally humiliating. If subjected to it repeatedly, the odds are good that, rather than continue to put up with it, most employees will eventually rebel, shut down, or move on. In this context, the old saying "People quit their bosses, not their jobs" has a powerful ring of truth to it, doesn't it?

So what's the point? Despite what legions of management consultants may claim to the contrary, I'm convinced that there really are only two management styles in use in the world of work: (1) command-and-control/carrot-and-stick and (2) Respectful Leadership. The first is considered disrespectful by most people; the second isn't. The first is also considered by organizational experts to be unsustainable, demeaning, and a waste of human creativity, generosity, and potential; the second isn't. Unfortunately, the first is very common; the second is relatively rare.

Respectful Leadership is defined as giving others—regardless of their (or your) rank or status—the same kind of genuine regard and consideration that you want them to give to you. If you boil it down, being a Respectful Leader is about following the Golden Rule: *"Do unto others as you would have them do unto you."* It's also about following the Platinum Rule: *"Do unto others as they would have you do unto them."* I would simply add that all of this "doing unto" needs to be done as respectfully as possible.

Respectful Leadership is not a new management style; it's as old as command-and-control/carrot-and-stick. It just takes a bit more intentionality, emotional intelligence, and conscious, consistent effort to do it sincerely and effectively.

Respectful Leadership is also sometimes known as "Servant Leadership," which is the practice of leaders serving as stewards or caretakers of their organizations and the people who work there. To me, the term Respectful Leadership seems more expansive than Servant Leadership, because being respectful is something you can practice all of the time—at work, at home, anywhere—and because using the word "servant" could be considered disrespectful.

Fortunately, these days, Respectful Leadership—as a practice— is more visible than ever before. This is partially due to the Conscious Capitalism movement, which has core tenets and principles that are closely aligned with the premise of Respectful Leadership. If you're not familiar with Conscious Capitalism, I strongly recommend you learn more about it. I am convinced Conscious Capitalism and Respectful Leadership have the power to transform our work world for the better, far more effectively and comprehensively than any other business movements that have come before.

It may not come as a surprise to learn that practicing Respectful Leadership is personally uplifting, motivating, and ennobling. There's something very satisfying that comes from treating others with respect and being respected in return. Leaders who practice Respectful

Leadership find that they are more at peace with themselves and feel more self-confident and resilient in times of crisis. They are better able, as the old saying goes, to keep their heads while others around them are losing theirs.

Respectful Leadership is also contagious. It appears that when one leader starts treating employees with respect and receives good results in return, others pick up on the trend and start emulating the behaviors. Managers start treating employees more respectfully; employees start treating each other and customers more respectfully; and pretty soon, a cultural shift occurs. My colleagues and I are convinced that once a majority of people (roughly 60 percent) within a particular organization practice Respectful Leadership consistently with integrity, then most others will follow suit or self-select out. It's entirely possible, with concerted and intentional effort over a period of time, for a few leaders to turn a disrespectful culture into a respectful one, with positive and sustainable outcomes. We've dramatized this idea in our fable in this book.

The primary story of *The Respectful Leader* revolves around two people: Des, the brand-new CEO of COR-Med, and Grace, who works in the company's maintenance department. Des's job is to "fix" COR-Med, to turn it around, to reduce expenses, and to make it, its products, sales, and profits better and sustainable. Grace's job is to fix COR-Med's building—specifically its old HVAC system—and keep it up and running.

The primary tool Des uses to try to do his job is command-and-control/carrot-and-stick management, which predictably causes some members of his leadership team to feel disrespected, to be disrespectful in return, and to eventually rebel. Another member of Des's leadership team, Spec, who is the head of R&D, openly engages in disrespectful behaviors in order to get his way. As for Grace, she consistently relies on one tool—an old but reliable pipe wrench—to get her job done.

Unlike Des and Spec, Grace also consistently uses another old tool, respect, whenever she interacts with anyone in the company.

She consistently treats everyone with respect and insists upon being respected by her bosses. Even though she is a maintenance worker, Grace is able to make a powerful, positive difference at COR-Med. Fortunately for Des, her successful use of respect catches his attention. Facing utter disaster, with few other options, he decides to give respect a try, and it works.

The moral of the story is simple: Respectful Leadership may be an old and relatively simple leadership style. But it's also a tried-and-true, highly effective management tool. If you want to be respected and gain personal satisfaction from being respectful; if you want to successfully influence the people you lead without micro-managing them or using intimidation or humiliation; and if you want to obtain positive, measurable, and sustainable business results, then Respectful Leadership is for you.

Concepts, Tools, and Techniques

Brief Questions and Answers About Respectful Leadership

What Is "Respectful Leadership"?

Respectful Leadership is the practice of giving others—regardless of their (or your) status, rank, or position—the kind of sincere, genuine regard and consideration that you want them to give you.

What Are the "Big Ideas" of Respectful Leadership?
- The Respectful Leader is the respected leader.
- Respectful Leadership is contagious.
- Respectful organizational cultures have positive, sustainable business results.

What Are the Seven RespectfulDo's?
1. Be the First to Respect
2. Practice Regular Respect
3. Be Respect-Worthy

4. Look for Diamonds in the Rough
5. Get Your Shift Together
6. Nip Disrespect in the Bud, Respectfully
7. Offer a Full Apology for Disrespect

What Are the Five RespectfulDon'ts?
1. Don't Try to Stop Disrespect with More Disrespect
2. Don't Tolerate Disrespect
3. Don't Be Distracted
4. Don't Minimize the Power of Respect
5. Don't Stop Practicing Respectful Leadership

How Will I Personally Benefit from Practicing Respectful Leadership?
1. You will be more respected.
2. Your team will be more respectful, productive, collaborative, trusting, loyal, and willing to go the extra mile when the going gets tough.
3. You'll be more resilient and better able to manage others during times of crisis.

4. You will experience greater composure, confidence, and satisfaction at work and in life.
5. You will be better able to make a positive difference with others.

What Are the Top Organizational Benefits of Respectful Leadership?

1. Increased collaboration, innovation, and productivity.
2. Increased candor, trust, honesty, and integrity.
3. Increased employee engagement, loyalty and willingness to go the extra mile in times of crisis.
4. Stronger, more resilient teams.
5. Increased likelihood of better decisions, results, and outcomes.
6. Reduced finger-pointing, turnover, conflict, and complaints.
7. Increased willingness to "own" mistakes and fix them.
8. Increased sense of camaraderie and positive organizational culture.
9. Better, stronger, more positive, and productive relationships with customers, vendors, partners, and the community.
10. A reputation as being a "great place to work" and a great organization overall.

The Seven RespectfulDo's

The Seven RespectfulDo's are the foundational practices of Respectful Leadership. When intentionally practiced together in a sincere and genuine manner, the Seven RespectfulDo's combine to become a powerful and highly effective way of operating and managing yourself when interacting with others, including your employees, your colleagues, clients, and bosses, even with your friends and family or complete strangers! The Seven RespectfulDo's will support you in consistently and positively influencing others without intimidation or humiliation.

Of course, if you wanted to, you could practice one or two of the RespectfulDo's and get some positive results, just like doing one or two specific physical exercises at the gym might help you build up your biceps or your back muscles. But this scattershot approach won't necessarily lead to people respecting you overall or to you being highly influential. However, if you genuinely and sincerely engage in all seven of the RespectfulDo's on a consistent basis, you will be respected by just about everyone.[*]

RespectfulDo #1. Be the First to Respect

Respectful Leaders offer others respect first; they don't wait to be treated with respect before being respectful.

One of the easiest ways to demonstrate that you have respect for people when you first meet them is to smile, make appropriate eye contact, use their surnames or *Sir, Ms., Mr.,* or *Ma'am,*[**] If you work with the military, police, or firefighters or around people who do, you'll usually hear them using this language all of the time, even when talking with civilians. While it may be hard to accept, you're not lowering your status in the eyes of others by acknowledging a subordinate's presence and calling him or her *Sir, Ms., Mr.,* or *Ma'am.* It is a simple sign of respect; it often feels good to do it; and most people like to be on the receiving end of it, but only if it's sincere.

In Chapter One of our story, Rita repeatedly called Des—who had just joined the company—"Mr. Hogan." When he asked her why she did that, she replied "out of respect." Rita's thinking: "He's my new boss and it feels 'right' and appropriate for me to be more formal with him." She was uncomfortable when Des asked

---

[*] Sadly, there are a few people in this world who, no matter how they are treated, find it impossible to behave respectfully. Do your utmost to avoid these people, they could hurt you in many ways.

[**] "Ma'am" is a complex appellation. In some places its use is entirely acceptable; in other places only the elderly are called "ma'am." Check to see whether it's in common usage in your area. When in doubt, stick with "Ms."

her to call him by his first name. You probably noticed Grace also called Des "Mr. Hogan." Her thinking is the same as Rita's. Even when he was openly disrespectful to her, Grace continued to use the more formal "Mr. Hogan." Admirable consistency.

Now, there's no question that our workplaces have become more and more informal, especially when it comes to the way we communicate with each other and the way we dress. This informality can break down silos and hierarchies, enabling many of us to feel more comfortable and willing to collaborate. It's easier to work with people we consider our equals.

But if Respectful Leaders are the first to respect when meeting someone new, they are setting a respectful tone for the relationship from the outset. Respectful Leaders signal that they are going to treat everyone, no matter their status or station in the world, with respect. This is a powerful first message to send, and it will most likely generate respect in return.

There's also a common belief in many cultures that "respect has to be earned," that people have to do and say things that we find respect-worthy in order to earn our respect. You may believe this yourself.

But for leaders, the "respect has to be earned" mindset is counterproductive for a number of reasons. First, it puts the employee, especially a new employee, at a disadvantage. Unless you've been extraordinarily explicit right at the beginning of the work relationship, your new employee is simply not going to know about all of the behaviors and language that you find respect-worthy. And you cannot assume that everyone is in common agreement on what is and isn't worthy of respect and walks in the door on the first day knowing exactly how to behave.

Second, even if you gave them your personal list of respect-worthy behaviors, new employees will be tripping all over themselves trying to meet your expectations, while at the same time trying to learn how to do their jobs properly, fit into the culture, and so forth. It's simply too much to ask of a new employee.

Third, when you insist, as Spec did in our story, that respect has to be earned, then isn't the opposite true? Don't you have to earn your employees' respect, too, or are you exempt from your own rule because you're the boss? To be blunt, to say that employees have to earn your respect, but you don't have to earn theirs, would be hypocritical and disrespectful. It would be implying that you are somehow better than they are, superior, someone who must be respected simply because of your position or status. There was a time, perhaps over a hundred years ago in Edwardian England, when this attitude might have been considered appropriate, but not anymore. In fact, given the expectations of today's Millennials, who will soon make up the majority of the workforce, the "respect has to be earned" mindset is completely counterproductive.

Of course, there are still some cultures, like the military and some very traditional organizations, in which leaders believe that the lower ranks must earn respect. But the Respectful Leader understands that the "respect has to be earned" mentality is disrespectful on its face. Instead, they give everyone the benefit of the doubt, regardless of status, and treat them with respect from the very start of the relationship.

Bottom Line: Respectful Leaders are the first to respect.

RespectfulDo #2. Practice Regular Respect

When we were very young, most of us were taught about manners, also known as "common courtesy." We were taught, for example, to smile when we meet or see someone, to say "Good Morning" or "Good Afternoon," 'Hello" or "Goodbye," or "Have a nice day," "Please," and "Thank You," in a pleasant and respectful manner. The Respectful Leader engages in common courtesy on a regular basis with everyone and is sincerely intentional about it. We call this RespectfulDo #2, Practice Regular Respect.

In our story, you may have noticed that when he called Des on the phone Chuck never said "Good morning" or even "Hello." He usually didn't say "Goodbye" either. And during the first leadership meeting, no one actually greeted Des pleasantly or sincerely (except for Grace after the meeting broke up). They were all too busy being angry (Spec and Janet) or distracted (Matt) or disengaged (Karl). These are all examples of leaders failing to practice regular respect, and as a result, they tended to engender disrespect and disrespectful behavior in return.

Here's a short list of Regular Respect practices for the business world, which are really just common courtesies, that you need to engage in sincerely and consistently with everyone.***

- **Make Eye Contact.** Make appropriate eye contact when you encounter someone, followed immediately by . . .
- **Smile.** Smile genuinely when you encounter someone. Everyone feels better when people smile at each other. Then add . . .
- **Greet People.** Say "Good Morning," "Good Afternoon," "Good Evening," or "Hello" to everyone in a pleasant and genuine manner.
- **Hold Doors.** Hold open a door for others, regardless of who they are. Thank them when they hold the door for you.
- **Use *Sir, Ms., Mr.,* or *Ma'am.*** During the early stages of a relationship, use Sir, Ms., Mr., or Ma'am and the person's surname in a genuine and cordial tone when speaking with him or her. Again, be aware of regional/organizational differences on the use of "Ma'am."
- **Say *Please* and *Thank You.*** Whenever you make a request of anyone, always include the word *please*. Whenever someone responds in the affirmative and/or honors your request, say *thank you.*

***Be aware that although most of these common courtesies are considered respectful in most parts of the world, different cultures from your own may have different interpretations and expectations. When in doubt, ask a local.

- **Say *Excuse Me*.** Say *excuse me* or *pardon me* sincerely when you mistakenly bump into someone or step in front of a person at the store. Say it when you absolutely need to interrupt someone, but interrupt others as little as possible.
- **Check Before You Jump In.** When calling or approaching someone and you don't have an appointment, greet the person and then politely ask, "Do you have a moment?" before you jump into your question or issue.
- **Re-Check.** When arriving at a meeting or calling someone at a time that has been scheduled in advance, ask "Is this still a good time?"
- **Be on Time.** Always be on time. Lateness is considered by almost everyone to be disrespectful. Leaders who are habitually late are sending the message that they believe their time is more valuable than that of others. Even if you believe your time is more valuable, others feel disrespected by that attitude. You won't be respected if you're late on a regular basis. We've found that even the busiest Respectful Leaders are able to be where they need to be on time. Think about it: if you're the boss of the bosses, you have more control over your schedule than anyone else has.
- **Let Them Know You'll Be Late.** If you're going to be late to a meeting, call in before the start time and let people know. When you arrive late, apologize sincerely. Don't make excuses (even if the traffic was horrific), just apologize.
- **Listen Attentively.** Attentively listen and wait for others to finish speaking before responding.
- **Apologize for Interrupting.** Say "I'm sorry to interrupt" in a genuinely apologetic manner when it's absolutely necessary to interrupt someone (again, avoid interrupting whenever you can).
- **Apologize When You Don't Understand.** When you don't understand or are confused by what someone has said, say "I'm sorry, I don't understand." Then allow others to restate their points or positions without interruption.
- **Mirror Back.** When you do understand, it's helpful to "mirror back" what others have said so they know that their ideas and perspectives have been heard and clearly understood.

- **Replace *but* with *and*.** Replace the word *but* with the word *and* as often as possible. When we use the word "but," we tend to negate the other person's point. This is disrespectful. Even if we disagree with the idea, using the word "and" enables us to get our point across without others feeling disrespected or contradicted.
- **Keep Your Distance.** In the workplace, it's best to limit physical contact to handshakes, unless you know someone really well and both of you are completely comfortable with a quick, light hug.
- **Avoid Certain Topics.** The age-old advice to *avoid talking about sex, politics, or religion at work* is still valid. However, these days, with news about these topics screaming at us from every tiny screen, it's much harder to stay mute. The reality is, most of us have very strong opinions about these topics and, in today's very diverse workplace, if we voice our opinions, they're bound to be overheard by someone who disagrees. If that person works for you, you've unwittingly widened the "trust gap" between you.
- **Keep It Clean.** Most everyone likes a good joke or funny quip now and then; they can lighten the mood, reduce stress, and increase bonding. The problem is that what's funny to you may not be funny to someone else. Be very careful when telling jokes or making remarks around race, gender, sex, age, nationality, regionalisms, sexual orientation, and intelligence, as you run a good risk of offending someone.

Bottom Line: Respectful Leaders practice engaging in regular respect sincerely and consistently.

RespectfulDo #3. Be Respect-Worthy

While you may believe others should treat you with respect because of your status, authority, or position, you can't expect that they automatically will. The Respectful Leader makes an ongoing effort to be worthy of others' respect.

In our story, many of the characters, including Des, failed to comport themselves in ways that most people would consider to be respect-worthy. Des, for example, lied to his customer, commanded and controlled, and openly yelled at his colleagues. Others, like Spec, seemed to be disrespectful on purpose and refused to take responsibility for their behavior. Still others shut down, checked out, or walked out of meetings abruptly. Also, some members of the leadership team—especially Spec and Matt—frequently used foul language. And a number of leaders were playing favorites and overlooking the disrespectful behavior of rainmakers and internal VIPs.

Here's a breakdown of leadership behaviors that most people find respect-worthy:

Be Honest. Obviously, lying to people is not respect-worthy. But plenty of leaders try to get away with it, for various reasons. The problem for them is that most people have what I call a "built-in B.S. detector"; they know when their boss is slinging them a line of baloney. People don't feel respected when they sense they're being lied to by their leaders.

You've probably heard the old saying that "honesty is the best policy." There's a lot of wisdom in this, partly because when you're honest most people sincerely appreciate it and are more willing to help you solve problems as a result.

In the middle of our story, Des visits the manufacturing area and does his best to be honest with the employees he meets there, even though his news is not particularly good. They responded appreciatively and respectfully. We can tell you from experience, from working with hundreds of companies, non-profits, and government agencies, that when leaders are as honest and open as they can be about what's going on, they are more respected and more trusted.

Follow Through. Another part of being respect-worthy is simply doing what you say you're going to do; following through on your commitments. No one respects leaders who break their promises. In fact, it is more respect-worthy not to make a commitment in the first place than it is to make a commitment and fail to honor it.

In our story, Des is forced to admit to his customer that he can't honor COR-Med's commitment and asks for more time. Fortunately, his customer gave him even more than he asked for. Most customers would not be so generous with a vendor that doesn't follow through on commitments. The same goes for employees and leaders. If employees find that the boss doesn't follow through, they'll eventually lose respect for the boss and look for work with a boss who does.

Be Fair. The Respectful Leader is consistently fair to everyone and avoids playing favorites. I've worked for managers who've played favorites—in fact, some of them made me their favorite!—and I didn't respect them for it.

In our story, it eventually became clear to Des and everyone else that COR-Med's success depended very much on Spec. Because of this, Des seriously considered overlooking Spec's disrespectful behavior, regardless of how destructive it was. Unfortunately, this kind of favoritism is very common in many organizations where the disrespectful behaviors of rainmakers and purported geniuses are given a pass by leadership because these people are considered invaluable. This kind of favoritism is not respect-worthy, to say the least.

Eventually, Des realizes that favoring Spec and allowing him to get away with disrespectful behavior is too costly to the organization. After a very concerted, responsible, and eventually unsuccessful effort to encourage Spec to change, Des is forced to let him go.

Respect-worthy leaders also go out of their way to hold everyone to the same expectations and standards. Most employees respond really well to a boss—even a very firm, no-nonsense kind of boss— who treats everyone in a consistently fair manner. If you couple this fairness practice with all of the other RespectfulDo's, you'll be well on your way to being respect-worthy.

Curb the Cursing/Name Calling. When it comes to cursing and swearing, most people—even those who use foul language themselves—generally have little respect for leaders who swear on a regular basis, especially if it's directed at others in the heat of anger.

And they definitely don't respect senior executives who yell and swear and call people ugly, disgusting names.

Even though you, and perhaps a few of your close colleagues, may personally be comfortable with these behaviors, it's imperative that you acknowledge that there are a significant number of people who are not, as they find them disrespectful. They don't consider these behaviors respect-worthy. Leaders who curse and swear at others may be feared, but they are not respected.

Now, of course, using a swear word when you stub your toe is usually understood and quickly forgiven by almost everyone. But cursing at someone or calling someone an ugly name is usually not. If you must swear, keep it about inanimate things and lousy situations, not people. And keep it quiet and to a minimum.

Be Clear. Most employees appreciate clarity from their bosses: they want to know what the goals are, how success is measured, and expected due dates and then be allowed to get on with achieving them as best they know how. Unfortunately, in the fog of busyness and multitasking, sometimes we're not as clear as we could be; we assume that our employees know what we want. As we all know, assumptions can get us in trouble. Or, the reverse is true, we think our employees need to be told exactly what to do and how to do it. This is, of course, what micro-managers believe.

The Respectful Leader offers clarity, but not every tiny detail, and opens the door for employees to ask questions without being worried that they'll be perceived as ignorant or needy.

Cultivate Patience. There's no question that in today's hyper-competitive business world, leaders everywhere are under enormous pressure to get things done very quickly. Unfortunately, this pressure is pushed on down into our organizations to the point where everyone is harping on everyone else to work "faster, faster, faster!" This approach can produce short-term results, but in the long run, it's exhausting and unsustainable.

The Respectful Leader understands that each person works best—and makes fewer mistakes—when allowed to work at the pace of his or her own choosing. Sure, some people will try to take advantage of a patient boss. But in a truly respectful culture, most people will willingly step up their pace when they see a genuine need to work fast. Cultivate patience; let people work at their own pace; set reasonable timeframe expectations; and trust that they'll produce for you. They will.

Bottom Line: The Respectful Leader consciously practices being respect-worthy.

RespectfulDo #4. Look for Diamonds in the Rough

While it may be easy to identify others' faults, it's also fairly easy to look for the good in them, too, if we want to. This RespectfulDo practice is called "looking for diamonds in the rough." Respectful Leaders consistently look for, find, and acknowledge those qualities, skills, and perspectives in others that are worthy of respect. They encourage others to do the same.

The impact of this particular RespectfulDo is phenomenal. When people feel genuinely respected and acknowledged for their positive qualities, skills, and behaviors, they feel proud of themselves; their self-confidence is boosted, and their overall attitude is positive and energetic. People who feel respected are much more loyal and willing to go the extra mile when times are tough.

In our story, Spec openly attacked Janet for what he thought were her failings. As far as he was concerned, nothing she did was of any value to him and what he needed to do for the company. And yet, Karl, Matt, and Des all thought Janet had important skills and knowledge, and they told her so. But it wasn't nearly enough to counter Spec's openly disrespectful behavior toward her, so she quit.

Later on in the story, Des told Spec he respected him as an engineer, but that his disrespectful behavior had to stop and that he needed to apologize for it. In the final analysis, you'll notice that Spec wasn't able to influence Janet (or anyone else) with his disrespectful approach, while Des was able to influence Spec—especially in terms of completing the Emperor prototype. He told Spec that he genuinely respected him for his knowledge, expertise, and experience. That's called looking for diamonds in the rough. In Spec's case, there was a lot of rough.

You need to be particularly intentional about looking for and acknowledging diamonds in the rough. You need to do it with everyone, not just your superstars. Each and every person in your organization brings something of value—usually it's a skill, experience, and/or the way he or she treats people—even if these things are not readily apparent or generally acknowledged by others. It's part of the Respectful Leader's job to ferret out those valuable attributes and behaviors in everyone and to acknowledge them in a meaningful way. There's nothing manipulative about this, as long as it's genuine and sincere.

Bottom Line: Respectful Leaders look for diamonds in the rough.

RespectfulDo #5. Get Your Shift Together

Shift happens! If you're a leader, you know problems and challenges are going to be brought to your attention all the time. You will react to them with shifting types, degrees, and intensity of emotion. You need to stay mindful of your shifting emotional states and do your best to "get your shift together" before reacting.

In our story, as Des was bombarded with more and more bad news about COR-Med, he became increasingly tense, frustrated, and worried. Eventually, he vented that frustration on his team and on his family, with severely negative consequences.

Part of being a Respectful Leader is ensuring you don't take out your anger and frustrations on others. The Respectful Leader uses various coping techniques to effectively manage shifting emotions. For example, early in the story, after Spec left the leadership meeting in a huff, Janet asked Des whether he would give her a moment to take a walk to clear her head, before going on with the meeting. This was a smart idea, because neuroscience tells us that a short walk outside in natural, full-spectrum light (even on a cloudy day!) can significantly elevate our negative moods. It's a shame that Des wouldn't allow her to do it.

There are plenty of other ways to get your emotional shift together. Sometimes, allowing yourself to take a very deep breath or two is all it takes. Or try standing up if you're sitting, or sitting down if you're standing, in order to change your blood flow and energy level.

Still another way to get your shift together is to find a "vent buddy," someone you can go to privately, close the door, and just vent in front of without fear that the person will try to solve your problem or blab what you've said around the organization. A good, reliable vent buddy offers a safe space for you to vent in, listens, and empathizes with your frustrations, and is invaluable.

Other ways to get your shift together include regular exercise, eating healthily, and maintaining a reasonable work-life balance. Sure, these are hackneyed recommendations, but they work, and they will help you build up your resilience and help you recover faster from bad and dispiriting news.

Bottom Line: Respectful Leaders do their utmost to get their emotional shift together, stay positive, and never take out their frustrations and anger on others.

RespectfulDo #6. Nip Disrespect in the Bud, Respectfully

The Respectful Leader consistently steps in and nips disrespectful behavior in the bud. This usually means taking people who have been disrespectful aside and respectfully informing them that their behavior is disrespectful.

In the story, when Des decided to go into the manufacturing area and speak with the line employees, he's confronted by Josh, making sarcastic, disrespectful remarks. Grace then gently tapped Josh on the shoulder, quietly asked for his help, and asked him to step aside with her. They eventually returned to the group, where Josh offered Des a full, public apology. Turns out that Grace had nipped Josh's disrespect in the bud, respectfully.

Later on in the story, when Des brought Kathleen into R&D to meet Spec and the other engineers, Spec was openly disrespectful to her. Instead of calling Spec on it in front of the group, Des—having learned from observing Grace—asked him to step aside and spoke to him privately about it.

One short and simple way to nip disrespect in the bud respectfully is to use the well-known SBI (Situation, Behavior, Impact) feedback tool. This tool was developed by The Center for Creative Leadership and is a very effective, and non-confrontational, way of giving someone feedback on behavior.

Here's how the Respectful Leader can use the SBI technique to nip disrespect in the bud. Once you've respectfully asked the person who's behaved disrespectfully to step aside with you and go to a private place away from public view, you then . . .

S: describe the **Situation** in which the disrespectful behavior took place,

B: describe, using factual and neutral language, the **Behaviors** you observed/heard, and then,

I: describe the **Impact** (also known as the "result" or "outcome") of those behaviors on you and/or others who were involved in the situation, especially in terms of how you "felt" when the disrespectful behavior occurred.

Usually, if you use neutral, fact-based and non-judgmental language and a calm, respectful tone during this process, the person will admit that you have correctly summarized both the situation and his or her behavior.

However, sometimes people may become defensive and try to justify behavior by making excuses, by blaming the situation itself or blaming others for "triggering" them, or by diminishing or disagreeing with your assessment of the impact of their behavior. At this point, what's most important is for you to "stay in the game" with people. Tell them that you understand what they're saying and then let them know that you don't think they intended people to feel disrespected, it's just that that's what you perceived and that it's possible others who were involved feel the same way as you do.

Once you've done this, it's more likely that disrespectful people will admit to that possibility and ask what you think they should do about it. Although you will really want to tell them what to do, such as suggesting "you should apologize," it's imperative that you resist this temptation. It's always best that people who've behaved disrespectfully develop their own response strategies. If they do, they're much more likely to claim it as their own and do it from an authentic place. Like children, people who feel "made to" apologize by their bosses are much more likely to do it insincerely and resentfully.

Instead, ask, "What do you think you should do?" Many people will respond by saying that they want to apologize, and in that case, you'll want to direct them to consider doing Respect-fulDo #7, "Offer a Full Apology for Disrespect."

Most people respond fairly well to the SBI feedback technique, but some do not. If you sense significant pushback, or if someone becomes upset and agitated or doesn't come up with the idea of apologizing, don't push it. Simply remind the person that you don't think it was their intention to be disrespectful, but that feelings of disrespect appeared to be the impact of their behavior, and leave it at that. After they've calmed down and thought it through (which they will, believe me), there's a good chance that they'll come back to you for further discussion. That's the time to coach them on what to do about it.

Bottom Line: The Respectful Leader Nips Disrespect in the Bud, Respectfully.

RespectfulDo #7. Offer a Full Apology for Disrespect

Sometimes our negative emotions get the better of us and we behave disrespectfully. That's called being human. As soon as you realize you've behaved disrespectfully (or when it's brought to your attention), you, as a Respectful Leader, need to offer a full apology for being disrespectful in a genuine and sincere manner.

In our story, after Josh behaved disrespectfully toward Des in the manufacturing area, and Grace took him aside to nip his disrespectful behavior in the bud, Josh returned to the group and offered a full and sincere apology to Des in front of everyone. Later on in the story, when Des realized how disrespectful he'd been to his own team, he offered them a full apology. This opened the door to them wanting to help Des and to ensuring COR-Med was successful. Des also apologized to his daughter, Megan, who in turn apologized to her mother.

A full apology has seven distinct steps, listed below. It's important to note that, in addition to completing each step, a full apology must be done honestly and sincerely without using phrases like "I'm sorry *if* I offended you" or "I'm sorry *you feel what I did/ said was offensive*" or "you're certainly *entitled* to your feelings." We call those kinds of words and phrases—especially the word "if"—"weasel words," designed to shift responsibility away from the person who engaged in the disrespectful behavior and onto those who felt disrespected. Using weasel words during an apology is insincere. Most people can sense that insincerity (remember the built-in B.S. detector?) a mile away and will dismiss or reject such apologies.

Interestingly, when a leader sincerely and fully apologizes for disrespectful behavior, there's plenty of evidence that most people will accept the apology and experience a lasting increase in their respect for that leader (as long as that leader doesn't repeat the disrespectful behavior). Unfortunately, many leaders find this idea hard to accept; they believe that if they apologize, people will consider them weak and/or that their apology will be taken out of context and used against them. So they simply don't apologize, no matter how disrespectful they've been. And while they may be feared by their employees as a result of operating this way, it's unlikely they'll be respected. It seems to me that going through life refusing to apologize for one's mistakes is not a good recipe for a happy life; it can take a serious toll on personal well-being and relationships.

Bottom Line: The Respectful Leader Makes a Full Apology for Disrespect.

The Seven Steps of a Full Apology. . .

1. **Admit It.** Admit, specifically, what you did/said and that you know it was disrespectful. *"I said/did XYZ and it was disrespectful."*
2. **Describe How It Hurt Them.** *"What I said/did hurt you and others because it . . ."*
3. **Make No Excuses.** *"I make no excuses for what I did/said; there are no excuses."*
4. **Apologize Sincerely, Ask for Forgiveness.** *"I sincerely apologize for what I have done and how I've hurt you and others. I ask for your forgiveness."* (Then, even if they don't forgive you . . .)
5. **Promise: Never Again.** *"I promise to never do/say anything like this to you or others again."*
6. **Offer to Make Amends.** Offer to make amends and ask for permission to make it right. *"I would like to make amends for what I've done and ask your permission to make it right. Here's specifically what I plan to do to make this right _____ ."*
7. **Start Immediately.** Even if they refuse to give you permission to make it up to them personally, go ahead and start doing the "right" thing with them and everywhere else in your life. You may get permission in the future.

Remember, your apology must be honest and sincere and come from a genuine place of wanting to make amends to the people you offended. In addition, never insist on or press them to accept your apology; doing so only makes them think you're only apologizing to relieve your own guilt. Rather, the true full apology is about them understanding that you fully own and sincerely apologize for something that you did or said that you know for a fact hurt them. You also need to thank them at the end for listening, no matter how they respond.

The Five RespectfulDon'ts

Before going into detail on the five RespectfulDon'ts, we want to make it clear that as consultants, coaches, and advisors, we would never want to fall into the trap of telling a leader to avoid doing something without recommending something else that they should do instead. As you'll see from the following, all of the RespectfulDon'ts have their RespectfulDo counterparts.

RespectfulDon't #1. Don't Try to Stop Disrespect with More Disrespect

Like respect, disrespect can be contagious. Sometimes, when people treat us disrespectfully, we are emotionally triggered and lash out with equally, sometimes even more, disrespectful behavior. This is the very human, fairly common, and somewhat understandable "fight fire with fire" reaction. The problem is that using disrespect to stop disrespect almost never works.

Why? Because when someone engages in disrespectful behavior, they're obviously not acting from the mature, patient, thoughtful, and reasonable part of themselves. Instead, they're being disrespectful as a result of some negative emotions, tendencies, frustrations, and biases that were ingrained within them in the past and that have now been re-triggered. In a way, they're in the grip of their emotions and can't manage themselves. This is not an excuse, just an explanation.

In our story, time and time again whenever Des grew frustrated and upset, he vented his emotions disrespectfully on others. And while he was doing it, he noticed that he was out of control, but didn't necessarily see this as a problem, or he couldn't help himself. This is very, very typical.

So, when a person is being disrespectful, he or she is usually worked up, a little out of control, and potentially itching for a fight. When someone is in this state, trying to stop that person from behaving disrespectfully by disrespecting them back is simply not going to work. It's going to make matters worse.

Here's a classic example: imagine you're in a meeting with your team and someone calls one of your customers a "total, freakin' ass****." Regardless of whether or not you—and everyone else in the meeting—agrees with this assessment, as a leader you know that this kind of disrespectful language is destructive and offensive. You want to shut it down immediately. But you've also been triggered; you really don't like it when your team members denigrate customers in public. So you react and shout at the offender: "Don't be a total, freakin' ass**** yourself! Don't talk that way about our customers!" The mood of the meeting immediately becomes tense. But, instead of addressing it, you try to move on.

Yes, you've succeeded in shutting down your team member's disrespectful behavior. But that person is likely to feel humiliated and be angry at and resentful of you for calling out the change to their behavior in public. That person is not going to be thinking about and regretting their own disrespectful behavior; instead, they will be focused on yours. Your disrespectful behavior has only compounded the situation, making it even more disrespectful.

The reality is, when we feel disrespected, the temptation to be disrespectful in return can be very strong, almost uncontrollable. But when we try to stop disrespect by being even more disrespectful, there's a significant risk the entire situation will spin out of control.

In the story, you'll remember that after Janet quit, Spec was openly disrespectful, claiming, "We're better off without her." Matt exploded at Spec and called him ugly names. A few moments later, Des responded to Spec's disrespectful remarks by angrily threatening to terminate him. Spec taunted Des to go ahead, and the tension quickly escalated. Later on, when Des's daughter, Megan, called her mother another ugly name, Des lost his self-control, yelled at her, and called her the same ugly name. In all of these cases, the people who felt initially disrespected were triggered, and their attempts to stop disrespect with even more disrespect failed. In all cases, the relationships were further strained and required more effort to mend.

In the case of the team member making disrespectful remarks about your customer, one respectful response would be: "Excuse me everyone, we need to be careful about how we talk about our customers. They're our bread and butter and we need to stay respectful no matter what." You'll notice that I suggest you use the words "we" and "our." This approach is inclusive of everyone, and it avoids singling out the disrespectful team member, making it less likely that person will feel humiliated and disrespected by you. It also demonstrates to the team that you can continue to behave respectfully, even when others aren't. Usually, decent people will realize they've made a mistake, apologize, and hope the conversation moves on. Of course, after the meeting, you can take that person aside and use the SBI technique with them. Remember, respect is contagious. In the final analysis, by staying respectful in the meeting, you've set a powerful, positive example for others to emulate.

Bottom Line: Respectful Leaders don't try to stop disrespect with disrespect. Instead, they will stay calm and respectful, de-escalate the situation, and eventually take disrespectful individuals aside where they can engage in RespectfulDo #6, Nip Disrespect in the Bud.

RespectfulDon't #2. Don't Tolerate Disrespect

Disrespect takes many forms. It could be as subtle as repeatedly interrupting people before they finish what they're saying, ignoring them, contradicting them, audibly yawning, having sidebar conversations while they're speaking, or making quiet, behind-the-back critical remarks or jokes about gender, experiences, skills, age, background, personality, or nationality. Blatant disrespectful behaviors include calling someone an idiot (or a host of other offensive names), cursing, slamming doors, flipping the proverbial bird, throwing things, pushing, shoving, humiliating, and threatening someone.

Unfortunately, too often, when people treat each other with disrespect in the workplace, leaders tolerate it and look the other way. Why? Partly because disrespect is considered by many to be in the eye of the beholder, dependent on our personal biases, preferences, upbringing, experience, tolerance level, and on what each of us consider disrespectful. The point is that there's no common agreement on what constitutes disrespect. But most decent, reasonable people—like Supreme Court Justice Potter Stewart who was struggling to define obscenity in 1964—will know it when they see it.

Even disrespectful people, after they've calmed down, can be coached to understand how their behavior might be considered disrespectful by others.

Another compelling reason many leaders may tolerate disrespect is because it's their boss or colleague engaging in it, and they feel powerless to stop it. This is very, very common and very sad.

Still another reason many leaders tolerate disrespect is because the disrespectful person is a serious rainmaker or VIP who is considered indispensable and/or is favored by senior executives who aren't necessarily the target of the disrespect.

In our story, Des was repeatedly frustrated by Spec's disrespectful behavior and yet, for quite a while, he did nothing about it, because he was more afraid of what would happen to COR-Med if he fired Spec than he was of the negative impact of Spec's disrespectful behavior on everyone who worked there. So, he tolerated it for too long.

Another reason many leaders tend to tolerate disrespect is because they're command-and-control/carrot-and-stick leaders themselves, and they honestly think disrespect is no big deal. They don't think it's nearly as serious nor as blatant as sexual harassment or as potentially damaging as physical violence. They think it's just boys being boys, girls being girls, and the way people have always treated each other. Heck, they may be saying to themselves: "I paid my dues. People disrespected the heck out of me as I came up through the ranks and I turned out fine." Employees, they may be thinking, need to grow a thicker skin and focus on their jobs and stop worrying about touchy-feely stuff like disrespect.

If you work for a boss who thinks like this, experience tells me you probably won't be working for the person much longer. If you're a colleague of someone who thinks this way, you can try to coach him or her, but it's unlikely you'll make much headway, if any at all. I've found that leaders who repeatedly tolerate disrespect are probably engaging in disrespectful behavior themselves, and they are not particularly open to feedback or coaching. That doesn't mean you should ignore it; you will need to use whatever influence and resources you can to make the situation better for all concerned.

Regardless of the reasons for tolerating disrespect, any leader with a modicum of decency and common sense will acknowledge that a disrespectful work culture can have a seriously negative impact on business relationships, customers, collaboration, morale, turnover, productivity, and so many other important aspects of the organization.

If you've been disrespectful yourself, you need to own it and offer a full apology for it. Respectful Leaders don't tolerate disrespectful behavior, not even their own, because the costs are too high.

Bottom Line: Respectful Leaders don't tolerate disrespect. They nip disrespect in the bud as soon as possible, and they offer a full apology for their own disrespect.

RespectfulDon't #3. Don't Be Distracted

Our portable technology is constantly demanding our attention. But if we allow it to distract us when we're supposed to be interacting with people who work with and for us, they feel disrespected. In our story you'll remember that just about everyone—especially Matt—is repeatedly distracted by digital devices. Des is annoyed by this behavior but, initially, he doesn't say anything to anyone about it, and he's the boss!

If you're going to be in a meeting (especially if it's one you called), then be "in" the meeting. Set the phone aside on "Do Not Disturb" and focus. If you've got truly urgent texts or emails that you have to respond to, then either drive the agenda forward, step out and manage them as quickly as you can, OR postpone the meeting entirely.

A colleague of mine deliberately sets aside three 15-minute periods—once in the mid-morning, once during lunch, and once mid-afternoon—specifically to interact with his smart phone. The rest of the time, he puts it in his briefcase set on "Do Not Disturb." He tells me that setting it on "Silent" is not enough, because he can still sense it vibrating. This may not be a strategy that's practical for you, but if you're deliberate and intentional about using the "Do Not Disturb" function, even if you keep your phone on your person, you will make progress on staying engaged.

Many of us also tend to be distracted by our technology while we're with family and friends. It's just as disrespectful as it is during meetings.

Bottom Line: Respectful Leaders don't get distracted; they practice Regular Respect.

RespectfulDon't #4. Don't Minimize the Power of Respect

There's an old saying: "When the going gets tough, the tough get going." I've modified that saying to: "When the going gets tough, people get tough on each other."

This means that sometimes, when there's a crisis at work that requires a response from the team, we'll push the need for respectful behavior to one side, minimizing its importance. We become so intent on trying to put the fire out that we do a little verbal self-justification dance that sounds like this: "There's a crisis! I don't have time to be respectful! People need to step up and stop messing around. I need to command and control them, kick their butts, whatever." This is exactly the disrespectful approach that Chuck recommended to Des early in our story, with disastrous results.

"But," you might be thinking, "I'll never be as bad as Des." OK, maybe not. And, yes, you can minimize respect and be disrespectful once or twice and the people you disrespect will perform. But they'll do so resentfully, and sooner or later, if you keep giving yourself permission to disrespect others, you'll be disrespectful more and more often, and people eventually won't perform for you anymore, because they've shut down, tried to undermine you, or have moved on.

Let's say you make a conscious effort not to minimize respect, but you slip up and are disrespectful in a real, no-kidding, crazy-massive, no-holds-barred crisis. Well, once the crisis has been averted with the help of the people you disrespected, if you're a decent person, you'll find yourself offering an apology. That's called RespectfulDo #7, *Offer a Full Apology for Disrespect*. There are seven steps in the full apology process; they involve real work, contrition, and ongoing effort. Isn't it smarter and more efficient to avoid minimizing respect in the first place?

If you consider it objectively for even just a moment, you'll begin to understand that respect is an extraordinarily powerful motivator and remarkably effective influencer. If we treat people with respect, even when the going gets really tough, people will step up and perform.

Bottom Line: The Respectful Leader doesn't minimize the power of respect, but consistently engages in the RespectfulDo's, no matter the crisis, no matter how difficult.

RespectfulDon't #5. Don't Stop Practicing Respectful Leadership

Once you've started practicing Respectful Leadership, you'll begin to see positive results, some of which will surprise you. Employees, colleagues, customers, and your bosses will notice, although they won't quite know what's changed about you unless you tell them. You'll be tempted to continue practicing being respectful, and that, of course, is a very good thing.

However, you've probably realized by now that if you stop being respectful, you will pay some kind of serious price for it, such as losing the respect of others—or losing them altogether.

Fortunately, practicing Respectful Leadership has many personal rewards, including greater self-control, satisfaction, confidence, and general happiness. These are powerful motivators for everyone.

In our story, Des met another CEO who had similar business challenges and people problems. One day, fed up with negative results, that CEO decided to stop being a jerk and, with the help of an executive coach, started practicing Respectful Leadership. The results, both professional and personal, were outstanding.

Unlike Des, that particular CEO is a real person—although out of respect for him, we won't say who he is. This CEO hasn't stopped being the Respectful Leader and tells us he's never been more successful or more satisfied.

Bottom Line: The Respectful Leader doesn't stop practicing Respectful Leadership, ever.

A Deeper Dive into Respect and Disrespect

The Two Types of Respect/Disrespect

Most people aren't aware that there are actually two types of respect. We call them *instant* and *developed*.

Instant respect (or *instant disrespect*) is an unconscious, instinctual reaction that usually occurs just a few milliseconds after coming into face-to-face contact with someone we've never met before.

This instant respect/disrespect reaction is almost always based on visible cues such as gender, race, ethnicity, age/generation, clothing (its condition and how its worn), facial expressions, body type and size, hair style, piercings, tattoos, and so on. Also, we might sense someone's energy level and mood when we first meet him or her or hear something in his or her voice, such as an accent or tone. Some or all of these cues will then almost instantly combine in our brains to trigger previously developed positive/negative biases within each of us, which then lead to an instant respect or disrespect reaction.

Here's an example of how this unconscious mechanism works. Imagine you're attending a public outdoor event—such as a street fair—filled with people milling around, visiting food stalls, listening to live music, buying gifts, etc. Now, imagine walking past a police officer in uniform who is calmly standing off to one side, smiling at everyone while observing the crowd. It's likely that, even if you don't know them personally, you would have an instant respect reaction to this police officer, out of respect for their work, uniform, position in our society, and because at the moment they seems helpful and friendly. You might even make eye contact, smile genuinely, nod, and say "hello."

Now roll back the clock for a minute and imagine that, in the past, you'd had one or more negative interactions with the police; encounters in which you were aggressively searched or arrested, or you felt treated very unfairly, dismissively, or disrespectfully. If this were your personal experience, it's more likely that you would have an instant disrespect reaction to the officer standing at the street fair, even if you'd never seen that particular officer before. You probably wouldn't do anything about your instant disrespect reaction, but it's very doubtful you'd smile, nod, and greet them warmly. Most likely you'd walk on by without making eye contact and quickly get yourself away from their gaze.

The same instant respect/disrespect mechanism comes into play at work. For example, if you meet a brand-new employee for the first time and they appear to you to be well put together, are wearing what you consider to be appropriate clothing, smells fresh and clean, and has a warm, friendly voice and a firm handshake, then you'd probably have an instant respect reaction to them. But, if they were dressed sloppily or had what you thought was a grating, nasal, or raspy voice and a limp or cold handshake, you'd probably have an instant disrespect reaction.

Again, in general, most of us are completely unconscious of this mechanism even though its constantly operating within us.

The second type of respect and disrespect is called *"developed respect/disrespect."* This type of respect or disrespect develops over time, as we learn more about someone's "invisible attributes" such as talents, skills, education, experience, political leanings, nationality, marital and parental status, religion, etc.

Going back to the workplace example: if you were to meet a new employee and have an instant respect reaction to them and then you got to know the person and learned about their experience, skills, and education and all of those things impressed you and/or were similar to your own, and you found the person to be consistently respectful and professional to you and others, and you also found that they honored commitments and did what you considered to be a "good job," then it's very, very likely that you would develop a high level of "developed respect" for that new employee.

But if the opposite were true, and over time you discovered you had very little in common and you weren't impressed by their experience, skills, or education, and they seemed to you to be disrespectful and unprofessional in interactions with you and others and didn't do what you considered a "good job," I can almost guarantee that you would develop disrespect for that new employee.

Understanding developed respect and disrespect is important because a mechanism inside each of us called "confirmation bias" makes it very difficult for any of us to change an opinion of a new employee. *Confirmation bias* occurs after we've made up our mind about someone, when we find ourselves continuously looking at and interpreting everything they say and do as confirmation of what we've already decided. It's as if we put on a specific pair of sunglasses every time we see that person, and we see everything they do only through those sunglasses. And we don't even realize we have them on!

Why is this so important? Well, if you've concluded that a specific individual is worthy of your respect, then you're probably not going to change your mind, even when confronted with clear evidence to the contrary. In fact, you'll probably dismiss the evidence as invalid or politically motivated. You might even aggressively defend the person you respect or excuse bad behavior as an anomaly, simply because changing your mind would mean admitting that you had misjudged someone or offered undue loyalty. That's very hard for most of us to do.

Conversely, if you've decided that someone is a jerk and not worthy of your respect, it would be just as hard to change your mind, even when confronted with a laundry list of examples of all of the respect-worthy things he or she might have done. Confirmation bias is a very strong, and yet almost totally unconscious, mechanism within each of us.

In brief, the two types of respect, *instant* and *developed,* and the mechanism called *confirmation bias* are constantly in play, unconsciously, in each of us. Part of being the Respectful Leader is being aware of these—and managing them accordingly.

Respect and Trust Go Hand in Hand

There are a great many solid and useful books and programs on teamwork and collaboration that make it clear that all really effective teams have high levels of trust. I agree completely. But, often as not, the terms "respect" and "Respectful Leadership" are not highlighted in these books and programs or, in some cases, even mentioned at all.

Why is this? It may be that some people find the concept of "respect" to be a little old-fashioned, quaint, or even just "a given." Except, of course, when there's a lack of it; then everybody's talking about it.

I would suggest that respect and trust go hand in hand, that you can't have one without the other.

Here's why. When you think about the people you work with and what you respect about them, you'll find yourself focusing on these three things:

1. Their experience doing what they do
2. Their skills and talents doing what they do, and
3. The way they interact with you and others.

When we're starting to work with someone, we're usually trying to size the person up in these three areas, to see whether he or she has the experience and skills to do the job, as well as the ability to get along with everyone who works there. This "sizing up" strategy makes sense because, generally speaking, these are the three areas—experience, skills, and interpersonal interaction—that are almost always in play in the workplace. At the same time, as we develop respect for people in these three areas, and they consistently meet or exceed our expectations, we start to trust them.

Here's a real-world example of how respect and trust go hand-in-hand.

For many years, my colleagues and I have provided leadership training to mid-level managers working in a global consulting firm in which client engagement teams are continually forming and disbanding. As a result of client needs, new team members come and go on a regular basis. During our program, we ask them to describe their assumptions about and expectations of their new team member, who is almost always someone they don't know.

Here's a paraphrasing of the response we get from almost every leader in this program:

"First, before I've even met the person, I trust that my boss has picked the right person for the role. In other words, I assume the new person has the required skills and experience that are needed to do the job, or why else would the boss bring that person onto the team? At the same time, I'm observing the person's behaviors, watching how he or she communicates and interacts with everyone else. If all of those things line up in a way that seems to serve the team and fit with how we already work together, then I'm going to start trusting that person. Eventually, if the person has stepped up and performed consistently and treated us all with respect, he or she will become a trusted member of the team."

My point is . . . yes, successful and effective teams have high levels of trust. But let's not forget that respect plays a significant role, too. Respect and trust go hand in hand. I'll be going into more depth on this idea in my next book, *The Respectful Leader on Teamwork,* due out in 2017.

Final Thoughts

It's probably safe to assume that if you've come this far into this book, then you actually do have a sense—or you've become aware by reading our fable—of how powerful, positive, and influential respect can be and how destructive, negative, and divisive disrespect can be. Perhaps you've realized that it's not in your best interests—or those of your organization, family, and friends—to engage in disrespect or to tolerate it anymore. Good for you! Awareness is half the battle.

The question is: What's your next step?

At the Gregg Ward Group, we'd rather you not learn how to be the Respectful Leader the way Des Hogan did in our story: the hard way. We recommend instead that you start by looking at yourself for a moment, taking stock of your own behavior, and comparing it to the Seven RespectfulDo's and the Five RespectfulDon'ts. Use our online assessment tool, found at www. RespectfulLeader.com to help you do this.

Then choose to practice one or two of the RespectfulDo's and RespectfulDon'ts, whichever seem easiest to you. Most people start with RespectfulDo #1, *Be the First to Respect*, and RespectfulDo #2, *Practice Regular Respect*, and quickly make these consistent practices. We've found that if you master a few of the "easier"

RespectfulDo's and RespectfulDon'ts first, you'll be more confident taking on the rest, until eventually you're practicing them all consistently. It usually takes from six months to a year of intentional effort to fully transform into a Respectful Leader. Of course, an executive coach can help you accelerate the process.

While you're transforming yourself, there's no reason in the world not to start spreading the concepts of Respectful Leadership throughout your organization. Talk about it with your employees and colleagues. Share this book; buy it for a disrespectful leader you know and surreptitiously leave it on his or her desk. Promote and engage in learning and development programs on Respectful Leadership. We'll be happy to help.

Respectfully Yours,
Gregg Ward and the Gregg Ward Group

Acknowledgments

Part of the practice of being a Respectful Leader is openly acknowledging the talents, skills, and efforts of those who've helped you reach your goals. There are quite a few people who've helped me reach the goal of writing this book and seeing it published, and they deserve all of the acknowledgment I can give them.

First, I'd like to thank Walter G. Meyer for his invaluable guidance, for sharing his impressive expertise and knowledge around all of the different writing styles that go into creating a book like this, for the many hours he spent reviewing, editing, and making suggestions, and perhaps most importantly, his follow-through in completely honoring every single commitment he made.

Second, I'd like to acknowledge and thank all of the great people at John Wiley & Sons, including Lia Ottaviano, Shannon Vargo, Peter Knox, Dawn Kilgore, and most especially Peter Knapp, who kept encouraging me to dream bigger.

Also, a thank you is due to the many Gregg Ward Group colleagues, associates, clients, and partners who've been supportive of me, including Donna Orlando, co-founder and COO of Orlando-Ward & Associates, Polly Croteau at Booz Allen Hamilton, Diana Stein of Beacon Training, Eric Murray at the U.S. Department of Labor, Kelly D'Souza and Carida Johnson at Kaiser Permanente, Kevin Rafferty—The Conscious Leaders' Coach, Lynn Coffman, Sandra Greefkes, Tom Stephenson, Michael Valentine, and Maurice Wilson, among many others.

I'd also like to thank the wise, funny, and creative Steve Saars, the CEO of Parallel Interactive Communications in San Diego, and his colleagues Patti Testerman and Sarah Glanz. I also want to acknowledge my talented video producer, Dinah Smith, videographer Tommy D., and everyone at Annie Jennings Public Relations in New York.

Since 2011, I've been part of an Authors' Mastermind group I co-founded with the author and speaker Cindy Burnham, who is also my closest colleague and a dear, trusted friend. Thank you, Cindy! This Mastermind group, which includes Jordan ("No-Nonsense") Goldrich, Will Headapohl, Walter Meyer, and Chris Witt, has consistently provided me with support, guidance, and encouragement. Thank you, fellow Masterminders!

Thank you also to all of our readers and testimonial givers: Chris Aaron, Joe Adan, Ken Blanchard, Eric Cornwell, Sally Daniel, Phil Dixon, Kenneth Freeman, Frank Ginsberg, Milton Green, John Kohut, Jack Lentz, Catherine Mattice, Matthew Rivaldi, Mark Schall, Raj Sisodia, and Nina Tassler.

I'd also like to acknowledge many friends for their support: Stephanie Trodello at Boston University's College of Fine Arts, Paul (Guitar-Man) Nichols, Peter Martin, and Mary Edmunds, Tom and Glenda Griesgraber, and most definitely Robert and Idette Makar.

I want to thank my family, including Dick, Sophia, and the entire Aaron clan; my late mother, Carol (love you, Mom, wherever you are); my steadfast and kind-hearted brother Gene Ward; my sister-in-law Jane Ahola; my sturdy nephews Jarred and Julian; and my amazingly smart, beautiful, talented, and spirited "step-daughters" Kate and Ali. I also want to thank my wonderful son, Leigh: kid, you always make me proud and keep me honest and in total wonderment at how awesome you are.

And finally, to my dearest Kathleen: thank you so very much for being such a positive, creative, generous, loving, and respectful partner. I am so incredibly lucky that you put up with me, keep me going no matter what, and most of all, that you love me.

About the Authors

Gregg Ward is the CEO of the Gregg Ward Group, a management consulting, training, and executive coaching firm focusing on Respectful Leadership, Emotional Intelligence, and Executive Presence. He began his career in the 1980s as a specialist trainer for The New York City Police Department. Since then he has developed, delivered, and facilitated thousands of keynote addresses and training programs for organizations ranging from global corporations to start-ups, and from large government agencies and universities to small non-profits. Gregg is also known as an international expert in the use of live, professional theater, interactive facilitation, and experiential learning as training tools on complex issues. He is an executive coach at the Center for Creative Leadership, holds the Board Certified Executive Coach (BCC) credential, and held the Certified Management Consultant (CMC) credential for over ten years. A graduate of Boston University's College of Fine Arts, and winner of the prestigious Fringe First Award at the 1991 Edinburgh International Festival, he also holds certifications in the *FIRO-B, DiSC, WorkPlace Big Five,* and *Leadership360* instruments. A former freelance journalist for various UK media, Gregg makes his home in San Diego. You can reach him at www.GreggWardGroup.com or www.RespectfulLeader.com.

Walter G. Meyer is an author, speaker, and expert on bullying, respect, and leadership. In addition to *The Respectful Leader,* he is the author of the non-fiction books *Going for the Green: Selling in the 21st Century* and *Day Is Ending: A Doctor's Love Shattered by Alzheimer's Disease*. He is also the author of the critically acclaimed and Amazon-bestselling novel *Rounding Third*. A graduate of the School of Communications at Penn State, Walt's feature articles have appeared in a host of national newspapers and magazines.

Additional Resources

For more information, please visit . . .

    The Gregg Ward Group
      www.greggwardgroup.com
      www.RespectfulLeader.com

Index

Page references followed by *fig* indicate an illustrated figure.